God's Thermometer

Tithing as Worship, Not Math

Joshua M. Sells, Esq., J.D., LL.M.

ISBN: 979-8-9931446-0-3

ABOUT THE AUTHOR

Joshua Sells brings a unique blend of professional expertise and personal testimony to his writing. He holds a Juris Doctor from Case Western Reserve University and an LL.M. in Taxation from Georgetown University Law Center. Over the course of his career, Josh has worked for two of the Big Four global consulting firms, advised Fortune 500 companies in complex mergers and acquisitions, and built a reputation as a trusted voice in the world of tax law. He has owned and led several businesses, and today he serves as the founder of a national tax law firm dedicated to "fighting the IRS" on behalf of individuals and small businesses.

Yet, for all of the titles, credentials, and worldly success, Josh discovered that none of it could satisfy the deepest need of his heart. Though outwardly accomplished, he inwardly wrestled with emptiness, discontentment, and striving. In 2018, Josh came to saving faith in Jesus Christ, and in 2021, he surrendered his life fully to Him. That moment of surrender reframed everything. His career, his ambition, and even his past successes found their rightful place under the Lordship of Christ.

Josh and his wife, Kailley, live in northeast Ohio where they are raising their seven children with the prayerful goal of passing on a Christ-centered legacy. Their home is a place of family discipleship, daily devotion, and the joyful chaos of life with a large family. Together, they faithfully serve at their local church, Community Baptist Temple, where they are actively involved in ministry and outreach. Josh's greatest desire is not that readers see his résumé, but that they see the grace of God that reached down into a driven, ambitious heart and brought lasting fulfillment.

In August 2025, Josh answered God's call to full-time ministry in evangelism, being sent out of Community Baptist Temple. Out of that call, Legacy Builders Press was born—not just as a publishing effort, but as a preaching, teaching, and writing ministry dedicated to proclaiming God's truth. Its mission is to provide biblically faithful preaching, resources, and books that equip believers to leave a Christ-centered legacy and to lift high the name of Jesus for generations to come. Through Legacy Builders Press, Josh writes to encourage others to build their lives on what truly matters—not on fleeting success, but on the eternal hope found in Christ.

"The greatest legacy I can leave my children is not my career or accomplishments, but a life surrendered to Jesus Christ. He alone satisfies, and He alone is worthy."

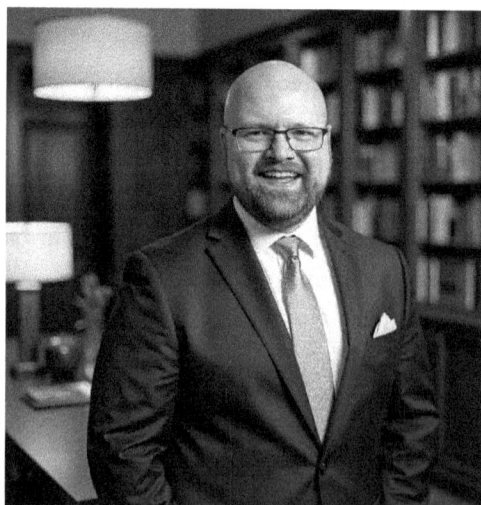

CONTENTS

MY TESTIMONY – AND HOW
YOU CAN KNOW CHRIST TOO

I was raised in a Baptist church from a young age. My parents were faithful to bring me to services, and I grew up hearing the Bible preached. As a boy of eight or nine, I had already "made a profession of faith" and been baptized. I had said the sinner's prayer, but looking back, I realize I didn't truly understand salvation or my own need for it.

One Wednesday night as a kid, I remember feeling a deep, unshakable conviction after the service. I tried to avoid everyone, even hiding behind my mom. My parents knew it was something spiritual and suggested I talk to my grandma Betty—a godly woman who walked with Christ. Pride kept me from it. I thought I could handle things on my own. That pride would follow me for years.

At fourteen, I made another profession of faith at teen camp. Not long after, my parents stopped going to church, and I did too. Through high school and into college, I drifted from God. Later, I got involved again in church life—

serving, attending faithfully—but I was never at peace about my salvation. Whenever an evangelist preached on eternity, I'd feel a surge of fear that if I died that night, I might not go to heaven.

Many nights I prayed privately, "Lord, if I'm not saved, save me." But nothing changed. I was embarrassed to admit my doubts to anyone. What would people think? That fear and pride kept me silent.

Then in 2018, my pastor, Mark O'Donnell, shared his own testimony. He said, "The devil may tempt you to doubt your salvation, but he'll never tempt you to get saved." That truth hit me hard. Why would the devil urge me to come forward in a church service? That was God's call, not Satan's. I realized I wasn't saved, and my pride was the barrier.

On Monday, I emailed my pastor asking to meet—partly so I couldn't talk myself out of it. By Wednesday night, I was ready. I knew all the Bible verses. I knew the gospel. But this time, I came empty-handed—no pride, no self-sufficiency, no terms of my own—just surrender to Christ. That night in August 2018, I trusted Him fully, and I have never doubted since.

It wasn't until later that I fully surrendered my life to the Lord, but my day of salvation was August 2018. Whether I only thought I was saved before as a child or truly was, I know this: that night I made an adult decision as an adult, and **everything changed**.

The Good News of the Gospel

Friend, maybe you've grown up in church. Maybe you've prayed before. Maybe you've even been baptized. But the question isn't what you've done—it's Who you're trusting. Salvation is not in a prayer, baptism, good works, or church membership. Salvation is in Jesus Christ alone.

The Bible says:

- We are all sinners. *"For all have sinned, and come short of the glory of God."* (Romans 3:23)
- Sin carries a penalty. *"For the wages of sin is death…."* (Romans 6:23a) This death is not just physical but eternal separation from God in hell.
- Jesus paid the price for our sins. *"…but the gift of God is eternal life through Jesus Christ our Lord."* (Romans 6:23b) *"But God commendeth his love toward us, in that, while we were yet sinners, Christ died for us."* (Romans 5:8)
- We must receive Him by faith. *"…if thou shalt confess with thy mouth the Lord Jesus, and shalt believe in thine heart that God hath raised him from the dead, thou shalt be saved."* (Romans 10:9) *"For whosoever shall call upon the name of the Lord shall be saved."* (Romans 10:13)

Salvation is not about fixing yourself first or bringing God an offer. It's coming to Him with nothing—empty-handed—and trusting in Christ's finished work on the cross.

Will You Trust Him Today?

If you don't know for sure that you're saved, I urge you: don't wait. Right now, you can pray from your heart something like this:

"Lord, I know I'm a sinner. I believe You died for me and rose again. I turn from my sin and place my trust in You alone as my Saviour. Please forgive me and save me. Amen."

There's nothing magical about the words—it's about truly believing and surrendering to Christ. If you will come to Him by faith, He will save you—just like He saved me.

CHAPTER ONE

THE GOSPEL HINGE: GLORY & THANKS

"Nothing reveals where your heart stands with God faster than what you do with your money."

I still remember my college professor in business school. His name was Harvey—I can't recall his last name, but he insisted we call him just "Harvey." He was a quirky guy, teaching a class called *Operations Management*. One day in class, he said something that stuck with me: *"Money is nothing but dirty paper."* He meant that money in itself has no magic, no life. It's paper passed from one hand to another. But in a society like ours, nothing reveals what's in the heart faster than what we do with that paper. That "dirty paper" is the quickest way to take your spiritual temperature. A local

3

pastor recently challenged that he wasn't concerned as much about what you were doing with the ten percent, as with the other ninety percent. What a thought!

That's why I believe money is tied to glory and thanks. In Romans 1, Paul explains the tragic hinge point where mankind turned from God: *"Because that, when they knew God, they glorified him not as God, neither were thankful; but became vain in their imaginations, and their foolish heart was darkened."* (Romans 1:21) Two refusals—no glory, no gratitude. Those weren't side issues; they were the hinge that swung the human heart into vanity, darkness, idolatry, and ruin.

The gospel reverses that hinge. To repent and believe is to turn and glorify God as God and to receive His mercy with thanksgiving. Gratitude and glory aren't extra works added to faith—they are the natural expressions of saving faith itself. But have you ever met anyone who was truly saved, but wasn't thankful for it in the moment of salvation? Impossible. Saving faith itself bows to God (glory) and receives His grace (thanksgiving).

And here's where the tithe comes in. Tithing is not just math. It's not a budget line. It is a thermometer. A thermometer doesn't set the temperature—it just reveals it. You don't make your heart right with God by writing a check, any more than you cure a fever by shaking the thermometer. But you can't hide the reading either. Money is visible. It's measurable. It touches everything. And nothing so quickly exposes whether your heart is alive with glory and thanks as what you do with God's portion (or any portion, actually).[1]

I can promise you something: a heart that is bowed before God in worship and overflowing with gratitude never struggles to "move a decimal point over" on the paycheck. In fact, I'll guarantee you that the people who glorify God and who live with thankfulness in their bones will, without calculation, end up giving well above ten percent. The tithe is the floor, not the ceiling. They don't even think of it as a debate. They rejoice in the privilege.

But the thermometer also works the other way. The closer a person tries to cut it down to the exact decimal, the "sicker" the heart may be becoming. If the tithe feels heavy, if you find yourself arguing, redefining, or resenting it— beware. The Pharisees were the classic example. They tithed down to the penny. If their increase totaled $483,572.04, I imagine they brought exactly $48,357.20—probably rounding down, keeping the twenty cents. Obedient in form, yes, but utterly cold in spirit. Jesus said in Matthew 23:23 that they tithed mint and anise and cummin, yet omitted judgment, mercy, and faith. They hit the number but missed the heart. Their thermometer reading was precise—and deadly.

That's the point of beginning. Before we chart out the biblical case that the tithe is pre-Law, under the Law, affirmed by Christ, and patterned by the apostles—before we walk through mechanics, objections, and real-world

---

[1] I fully understand that Romans 1 continues describing the unsaved. My point here is not that a believer who backslides and loses gratitude somehow forfeits salvation—we are sealed unto the day of redemption (Ephesians 4:30). But it is true that a saint can grieve the Spirit, lose thankfulness, and fail to keep Christ in His rightful place. The result is not the loss of salvation, but broken fellowship.

practice—we need to stop here at the heart level. Ask yourself:

1. Am I bowed before God, glorifying Him as God?
2. Am I thankful that He has entrusted me with His substance, which was never really mine?

If you are, the tithe won't be a debate. It will be the baseline. If you're not, then no argument in this book will feel persuasive until you settle the hinge.

So, let's start here: the gospel makes a man or woman new by turning them into someone who glorifies God and who overflows with thanks. The tithe is not about dollars and cents; it's about what those dollars reveal. It's a thermometer for glory and gratitude. And if you find yourself resisting it, don't start by moving the decimal point. Start by moving your knees. Bow low before the Lord. Give Him glory. Give Him thanks. Then bring the portion that is holy unto Him—with joy.

CHAPTER TWO

BEFORE THE LAW: THE TITHE BEGINS IN FAITH

"Before there was Law, before there was Mt. Sinai, God's people were already tithing—because worship always gives back to the Giver."

Before we even open up the word *tithe*, we need to start with a staggering truth: we don't own anything.

David said it this way: *"The earth is the LORD's, and the fulness thereof; the world, and they that dwell therein."* (Psalm 24:1) Everything—from the stars above to the soil under our feet—already belongs to Him. James echoes it: *"Every good gift and every perfect gift is from above, and cometh down from the Father of lights, with whom is no variableness, neither shadow of turning."* (James 1:17) Paul drives it home to the Corinthians: *"For who maketh thee to differ from another? and what hast thou that thou didst*

7

not receive? now if thou didst receive it, why dost thou glory, as if thou hadst not received it?" (1 Corinthians 4:7)

That's a humbling question. What do we really have that we produced out of thin air? Even our paychecks aren't really ours—we didn't create breath, or strength, or a brain, or raw materials. We've only rearranged what God already made. Even farmers don't make fruit grow; they just plant seeds into dirt they didn't create, water them with rain they didn't produce, and wait for a sun they don't control. Nothing is new under the sun—God made it all, owns it all, and in His wisdom lets us steward it.

That's biblical redistribution of wealth—not the socialist kind, but a divine one. We start with nothing, and He entrusts us with His abundance. The tithe, then, is not "giving something to God." It's returning to Him what was already His. That's why Leviticus calls it *"holy unto the LORD."* (Leviticus. 27:30)

Now, we have to pause and deal honestly with this. How are you with the truth that you own nothing—that it's 100% God's? Does that sit well with you, or does it bother you? Do you find yourself thinking, "Sure, God enabled me, but I'm the one who worked, labored, and sacrificed for what I have"? I know those feelings all too well. And if that's where you are, you have to settle that first.

Do you really know God? I'm not only talking about salvation—though that's foundational—but do you know Him in daily fellowship? Are you walking with Him in such a way that Psalm 24:1 doesn't end with a comma in your hearts? For years in my own life, that verse read, "The earth is the Lord's and the fulness thereof, and they that dwell

therein, but I worked hard… I put in the time… I built this."
I could quote the verse, but in practice I lived like it had an
unspoken add-on.

Here's the turning point: when you get serious about
your walk with God—real, personal Bible study, daily
fellowship, prayer from the moment you wake up, and
continual conversation with Him through the day until you
lay your head down—something shifts. We stop adding the
comma. The verse ends with a period. "The earth is the
LORD's and the fulness thereof." Period. No add-ons. No
disclaimers. No "but I…" attached. Everything we have is
His.

Until you see it that way, the tithe will always feel
negotiable, debatable, or heavy. But once Psalm 24:1
becomes a period in your heart, tithing becomes worship, not
math.

So, now that we've settled the heart issue—God owns it
all, period—let's roll up our sleeves and actually talk about
the tithe.

The First Mention: Abraham and Melchizedek

The first time the word *tithe* shows up in Scripture is
Genesis 14. Abraham has just rescued Lot, won a military
victory, and been blessed by Melchizedek—the mysterious
king-priest of Salem.

*"And he blessed him, and said, Blessed be Abram of the most high
God, possessor of heaven and earth: And blessed be the most high God,
which hath delivered thine enemies into thy hand. And he gave him
tithes of all."* (Genesis 14:19-20)

Stop and think about this: Abraham tithed **after** the blessing. He wasn't bargaining. He wasn't under command. He was overwhelmed by the God who had given him victory, and he returned a tenth as worship.

Who was Melchizedek? Hebrews tells us he was a "type" of Christ (Hebrews 7:1-3). Whether you take him as an appearance of Christ or simply as a divinely appointed picture, the point stands: Abraham gave the tithe to one who represented Christ Himself. In other words, tithing has always been about worshipping Jesus.

And note this detail: Abraham was blessed of the Most High God, and then gave tithes of all. That tenth was already God's—it came from God's hand through Melchizedek, and Abraham simply acknowledged it.

Jacob's Vow: A Voluntary Tithe Before the Law

The next mention of the tithe comes from Jacob in Genesis 28. After the dream at Bethel, Jacob makes a vow: *"And this stone, which I have set for a pillar, shall be God's house: and of all that thou shalt give me I will surely give the tenth unto thee."* (Genesis 28:22)

Notice the context: Jacob isn't yet calling the LORD "my God" (that comes later, after Peniel). But even here, Jacob recognizes a principle: if God blesses me, I will acknowledge it with a tithe. This wasn't an ultimatum, but a pledge of gratitude.

Again—no Law, no tablets, no Moses. Just a man responding to God's kindness with a holy portion.

Here's why those two examples matter: both Abraham and Jacob tithed centuries before Moses. Together, these two men—Abraham and Jacob—show us that the Law didn't invent the tithe; it simply codified a principle already alive in the hearts of God's people.

That means the argument—"tithing was under the Law, and we're under grace"—falls apart. Hebrews 7 even builds theology on Abraham's tithe, centuries later, to argue for Christ's greater priesthood. The New Testament doesn't dismiss Abraham's act; it magnifies it.

To argue that the tithe vanished with the Law is like getting pulled over for going 55 in a 35 zone and telling the judge, *"I wasn't going 55—I was only going 54."* Moot point. You were still speeding. Tithing existed before the Law, it was commanded during the Law, and it's assumed after the Law. Grace doesn't erase it—it raises the standard. If the Pharisees tithed down to the penny and were still rebuked for missing the heart, what excuse do we have under grace?

Hebrews 7: The Tithe That Lives On

If Genesis 14 gives us the first tithe, Hebrews 7 explains why that tithe still matters today. The writer to the Hebrews takes Abraham's moment with Melchizedek and builds a case that spans from Genesis all the way into eternity.

"For this Melchisedec, king of Salem, priest of the most high God, who met Abraham returning from the slaughter of the kings, and blessed him; To whom also Abraham gave a tenth part of all; first being by interpretation King of righteousness, and after that also King of Salem, which is, King of peace." (Hebrews 7:1-2)

The writer pauses here to describe Melchizedek: no genealogy recorded, no beginning or end written down, a king and priest all at once. He says Melchizedek was *"made like unto the Son of God; abideth a priest continually."* (Hebrews 7:3) The point isn't that Melchizedek was literally eternal, but that in the record of Scripture he appears without beginning or end, foreshadowing Christ's eternal priesthood.

Abraham's Tribute and Christ's Living Priesthood

Then the writer says something staggering: Abraham— the patriarch, the father of faith, the one who received the promises—paid tithes to this priest. And in so doing, Abraham acknowledged that Melchizedek was greater than him.

"And without all contradiction the less is blessed of the better. And here men that die receive tithes; but there he receiveth them, of whom it is witnessed that he liveth." (Hebrews 7:7-8)

Catch that: in Abraham's tithe, the writer sees a picture of Christ. Earthly Levites received tithes and then died. But Christ, our High Priest after the order of Melchizedek, still lives. And the language is present tense: *"[H]ere men that die receive tithes; but there he receiveth them."* Not "he received," past tense—but receiveth, now.[2]

---

[2] *Receiveth* renders a present active indicative, portraying the action as ongoing/characteristic. Even if a reader hears it as rhetorical, the contrast stands: *"here men that die receive tithes; but there he receiveth them, of whom it is witnessed that he liveth."* (Hebrews 7:8) In the flow of Hebrews 7:11–19, a change of priesthood entails a change of law; the point is not to reinstate Mosaic tithing but to relocate tribute under the better hope and the living Priest. We're not binding a new rule from Hebrews 7:8; we're identifying the Recipient/Owner.

That means every tithe brought by faith is received, not merely by men in a church office, but by the living Christ Himself. The act may look ordinary—an envelope, a check, a line on a bank statement—but heaven sees it as tribute offered directly to the eternal Priest.

This is why the "it was only under the Law" view is inadequate. Hebrews 7 anchors the tithe not in Levi, not in Moses, but in Abraham and Melchizedek—pre-Law, post-Law, and eternal. If anything, the New Testament elevates the tithe's significance by showing that it belongs to Christ's priesthood, not to a passing Levitical order.

Answering Common Objections to Hebrews 7

Someone will say, "Hebrews 7 doesn't command Christians to tithe." Fair enough. Hebrews 7 is not framed as a church bylaw; it is a Christ-exalting portrait of priesthood. But that is exactly why it matters. The writer takes Abraham's pre-Law tithe (Genesis 14) and—by the Spirit—sets it within the greater reality of Christ's priesthood: *"And here men that die receive tithes; but there he receiveth them, of whom it is witnessed that he liveth."* (Hebrews 7:8) The point is not merely, "Do this," but, "See to Whom this belongs." In other words, Hebrews 7 supplies the theological continuity: Abraham gave a tenth to Melchizedek, and that act is then taken up in Hebrews 7 and shown to be typologically located in Christ's living, non-Levitical priesthood. The practice is shown to belong to Jesus, not to a temporary, dying order.

Now let's be honest with the text. Verse 12 says that when the priesthood is changed, *"of necessity a change also of the law."* Verse 18 even speaks of "disannulling" a former command. I concede that gladly. The Levitical system as such is not carried forward[3]. What Hebrews does is relocate the logic of tribute from a dying priesthood to a living Priest. It is not, "reinstate Mosaic tithing," but, "recognize that whatever God's people set apart for His worship is now, by faith, received by Christ Himself." That is why I refuse to make Hebrews 7 a bylaw; I make it rooted in Christ Himself. The grammar serves the theology: what men *receive* and then die is contrasted with what He receiveth while He liveth— the act is lifted out of a time-bound Levitical frame and situated in the risen Priest. Then 1 Corinthians 9:14 supplies the church-facing ordinance (minister support), and 2 Corinthians 8-9 gives us the spirit of New Testament giving (cheerful, proportionate, abundant). Put together: not a re-imposed code, but a wise, time-tested floor that honors the same Owner and the same Priest.

Some object that Abraham's tithe was a one-off from battle spoils, not a paycheck (Hebrews 7:4). True—and that actually strengthens the point Hebrews is making. The writer

---

[3] Practices that predate the Mosaic law and are re-situated under Christ's priesthood supply a continuing pattern in principle unless the New Testament explicitly repeals, fulfills, or reframes them. In this sense, tithing is transferred in its recipient—from the Levites to the living Christ, and, by His ordinance, to those who preach the gospel (1 Corinthians 9:14)—not terminated. For a pre-Law pattern affirmed in the New Testament, see marriage as a creation ordinance (Genesis 2:24; Matthew 19:4-6; Ephesians 5:31-33). For repealed/fulfilled pre-Law practices, see animal sacrifices fulfilled in Christ (Hebrews 10:1-14) and circumcision set aside as a covenantal requirement (Acts 15; Galatians 5:2-6). The New Testament grounds the transfer of recipient (Hebrews 7:1-8, 12), ordains ministerial support (1 Corinthians 9:13-14), and shapes the posture of giving (2 Corinthians 8-9).

isn't giving a payroll manual; he's showing a hierarchy. Abraham—the patriarch and covenant head—acknowledges someone greater by giving him the first and best. That's why Hebrews stresses, *"the less is blessed of the better,"* and that Levi, *"in the loins of Abraham,"* paid tithes to Melchizedek (Hebrews 7:7–10). In other words, the episode isn't about the *source* of the increase (spoils versus salary); it's about the *posture* of the worshiper: the lesser honors the greater. The binding principle does not depend on whether the increase came from spoils or salary. It depends on the posture of the heart: the lesser always honors the greater. Genesis 14 is not a paycheck template; it is a worship template, and Hebrews lifts it into Christ's ongoing priesthood. The New Testament then applies the template to ordinary church life through regular, proportionate support of gospel workers (1 Corinthians 9; 1 Timothy 5:17-18). So, when I commend the tithe as a baseline, I'm not claiming Hebrews 7 legislates 10%. I'm saying the pattern belongs to Christ, the ordinance is supplied by Paul, and Christian liberty in 2 Corinthians 9 governs the spirit of it.

What about the present tense—*"he receiveth them"*? Even if a critic calls it rhetorical or literary, the theology remains: the tithe in Scripture is attached to a priesthood that lives. Levitical receivers "die"; Christ "liveth." The author's contrast lifts the act out of a merely Levitical, time-bound system and ties it to the risen Priest. This isn't just me being creative with symbols. The writer of Hebrews, under the Spirit, is interpreting Genesis this way on purpose. It's not human imagination—it's God's own explanation of what that moment with Abraham and Melchizedek really pointed to. I am not pulling a new law out of Hebrews 7. I am locating the tithe's owner—Christ—and then letting 1 Corinthians 9:14 provide the church-facing ordinance.

From Pattern to Ordinance: Paul's "Even So"

Where, then, is the New Testament precept? Paul gives it: *"Do ye not know that they which minister about holy things live of the things of the temple? and they which wait at the altar are partakers with the altar? Even so hath the Lord ordained that they which preach the gospel should live of the gospel."* (1 Corinthians 9:13-14) That *"even so"* is the binding ordinance that carries the temple support-pattern into the church.

Put simply: Hebrews 7 is the theology; 1 Corinthians 9:14 is the ordinance. Together they are stronger than either alone. Abraham's pre-Law tithe shows the pattern. Hebrews 7 shows it belongs to Christ's living priesthood. Paul's "even so" ordains its practice in the church.

Why This Matters for Us

Think about it: Abraham's tithe wasn't a tax, a duty, or a burden. It was a confession: *"God gave me victory, God blessed me, and I honour Him as greater."* Jacob's tithe at Bethel was a vow of gratitude. And Hebrews says those tithes point forward to something bigger—Christ, who still lives and still receives.

So, when we tithe, we aren't just funding a church budget. We are bowing before a greater Priest. We are saying with Abraham, *"Thou art greater."* We are confessing with

Jacob, *"Of all that Thou shalt give me I will surely give the tenth unto Thee."* And we are joining the testimony of Hebrews 7:8: *"he receiveth them, of whom it is witnessed that he liveth."*

That's not Law. That's worship. That's Christ.

This is why the "I don't tithe because we're under grace" excuse falls apart. Grace doesn't lower the bar. Grace lifts it higher. Under Law, Israel was commanded to tithe. Under grace, we get to tithe to a living Christ. Why would we argue for less?

The tithe existed before the Law, it existed during the Law, and Hebrews makes clear it exists beyond the Law. The only real question is: *what does my tithe say about my heart?*

So, let's tie this down.

God owns it all. Everything we have is received, not created by us. (Psalm 24:1; 1 Corinthians 4:7; James 1:17) The tithe is holy. It's His portion, not ours. (Leviticus 27:30)

The first tithes were pre-Law. Abraham and Jacob tithed out of worship and gratitude, not compulsion. (Genesis 14; 28)

Christ still receives tithes. Hebrews 7 says our High Priest lives and receives them now. (Hebrews 7:8)

That's the foundation. Before we ever step into Moses, Levites, or Malachi, the New Testament tells us plainly: tithing belongs to Christ. And when we tithe, we declare with our "dirty paper" what our lips ought to declare every day: *"Thou art greater. I glorify Thee as God. And I thank Thee for every undeserved gift."*

CHAPTER THREE

HOLY TO THE LORD: DEFINITION, DESTINATION, DESIGN

"The tithe was never left vague or optional—God defined what it was, where it went, and why it mattered: holy to the LORD."

By the time Moses receives the Law, the tithe is no longer just a voluntary act of worship from Abraham or Jacob. It becomes part of the covenant life of Israel—defined, directed, and designed by God Himself. The Bible always defines itself, and in Leviticus 27 we get the clearest definition of the tithe.

"And all the tithe of the land, whether of the seed of the land, or of the fruit of the tree, is the LORD's: it is holy unto the LORD . . .

19

[a]nd concerning the tithe . . . the tenth shall be holy unto the Lord." (Leviticus 27:30-32)

There it is: the tithe is a tenth, set apart, belonging not to the giver but to the Lord. Notice the word holy. Holy means "set apart," "not common," "belonging exclusively to God." The tithe is not ours to distribute where we please; it is the Lord's portion, already marked off as sacred.

Definition: All the Increase

The Bible does not leave the tithe vague. It defines it with precision. Leviticus 27:30 sets the foundation: *"And all the tithe of the land, whether of the seed of the land, or of the fruit of the tree, is the LORD's: it is holy unto the LORD."* The tithe wasn't partial, seasonal, or selective. It was *all* the tithe—whatever the land produced; the tithe belonged to the Lord. The scope covered every kind of increase: grain, fruit, flocks, and herds.

Deuteronomy makes the same claim of right, and sharpens the lens: *"Thou shalt truly tithe all the increase of thy seed, that the field bringeth forth year by year."* (Deuteronomy 14:22) Do you hear the clarity? Truly tithe *all*; the calculation is made "in the field," at the point of raw increase; and the rhythm is "year by year," regular and systematic. The tithe was not worked out later in the barn after reductions or adjustments; what came up, God claimed.

Numbers reinforces the picture when God assigns the tithe to the Levites: *"Behold, I have given the children of Levi all the tenth in Israel for an inheritance, for their service which they serve, even the service of the tabernacle of the congregation."* (Numbers 18:21) The tithe was not a voluntary gesture; it was God's designated portion—His means of sustaining His work and His reminder that He is the true Owner of the fields and the flocks.

Gather those strands and the picture is plain: the tithe covered everything—cattle, grain, fruit, wages. The principle is *all the increase*; in an agrarian economy that meant produce and herds. By principle, that extends to earnings/income in this generation. Think of it in today's terms: a ten-year-old who receives twenty dollars from Aunt Suzie for raking leaves has received an increase. A retiree who collects a monthly Social Security check has received an increase. A business owner who nets profit after business expenses has received an increase. God's definition is sweeping: *"all the tithe… is the LORD's."* (Leviticus 27:30) That alone demolishes the modern notion that the tithe is optional, negotiable, or subject to personal redefinition. If it is increase, then the tithe is His.

Destination: The House of the LORD

God never left the tithe to human discretion. He not only defined the tithe; He also directed its destination. The tithe had a God-ordained home.

Leviticus gives the definition—*holy unto the LORD*—and then the Law takes the next step: where does His holy portion go? Numbers answers it: *"Behold, I have given the children of Levi all the tenth in Israel for an inheritance, for their service which they serve, even the service of the tabernacle of the congregation."* (Numbers 18:21) The tithe was the supply line God ordained for those who served in His house. The Levites had no

21

inheritance of farmland. They could not plow and harvest for themselves. Their portion was the tithe, and through it God ensured that His house was never without ministers. This was not a "tip" to the Levites or a gift of goodwill; it was their inheritance by divine right.

God added a safeguard even here. The Levites themselves were commanded to tithe on the tithe: *"When ye take of the children of Israel the tithes… then ye shall offer up an heave offering of it for the LORD, even a tenth part of the tithe."* (Numbers 18:26) No one stands above worship. Even those who lived off the tithe still had to honor the Lord with His portion.

Deuteronomy then fixes the geography of obedience. The tithe was to be brought to a central place of worship, not left scattered at individual whim: *"But unto the place which the LORD your God shall choose out of all your tribes to put his name there, even unto his habitation shall ye seek, and thither thou shalt come: and thither ye shall bring your . . . tithes."* (Deuteronomy 12:5-6) The people didn't decide the destination. God chose the place where He set His name, and His people were required to bring their tithes there. It was not about personal preference; it was about obedience.

Deuteronomy 14 tightens the principle still more: *"Thou shalt truly tithe all the increase of thy seed, that the field bringeth forth year by year. And thou shalt eat before the LORD thy God, in the place which he shall choose to place his name there…."* (Deuteronomy 14:22-23) Again we hear the claim of right— truly tithe all—the location of calculation—in the field at raw increase—and the cadence—year by year. And when distance made it impractical to haul grain or cattle, God built in a merciful accommodation: *"If the way be too long for thee… then*

shalt thou turn it into money, and bind up the money in thine hand,
and shalt go unto the place which the LORD thy God shall choose."
(Deuteronomy 14:24-25) You could exchange produce for
money, but the holy portion still went to the place where
God placed His name. Destination was non-negotiable.

So the Law speaks with one voice: Leviticus declares the
tithe holy to the Lord; Numbers directs it to the Levites for
the service of His house; Deuteronomy commands that it be
brought to the place where God set His name—reckoned in
the field at the raw increase and brought with regularity, year
by year. The destination of the tithe was never a matter of
personal charity. It was bound to God's house, God's
ministers, God's worship, and God's chosen place.

Design: Sustaining God's Work

So why did God establish the tithe? He did not leave us
guessing. He told Israel plainly that the tithe was His
provision for His house and for those who served Him in it.
Numbers 18 gives the clearest statement: *"Behold, I have given*
the children of Levi all the tenth in Israel for an inheritance, for their
service which they serve, even the service of the tabernacle of the
congregation." (Numbers 18:21)

The Levites were unlike the other tribes. Every other
tribe received land as inheritance; the Levites received none.
Their portion was the Lord Himself and the holy service of
His house. To make that calling possible, God gave them the
tithe. This was not optional generosity; it was His design. The
tithe freed the Levites from having to plow fields or build
businesses on the side. Their calling was to minister, bear the

tabernacle, sing, teach, and serve in the holy things. The people's tithe sustained them so they could devote themselves wholly to the Lord's service.

And notice the deeper formation at work. God required the Levites to tithe on what they received: *"Thus speak unto the Levites, and say unto them, When ye take of the children of Israel the tithes… then ye shall offer up an heave offering of it for the LORD, even a tenth part of the tithe."* (Numbers 18:26) No one is exempt from worship. Even those who lived off the tithe had to acknowledge God's ownership. The design of the tithe was not only financial; it was spiritual—a rhythm of humility, dependence, and gratitude woven into the nation's worship.

Leviticus 27 reminds us again that the tithe was *"holy unto the LORD."* It was not common money for common use. It was set apart, consecrated, devoted entirely to God's work. By declaring it holy, God established that the tithe was never a matter of "what do I feel like doing with my resources?" The design was clear: His portion, for His house, through His servants.

Deuteronomy 14 ties the design to worship and discipleship: *"And thou shalt eat before the LORD thy God, in the place which he shall choose to place his name there, the tithe of thy corn, of thy wine, and of thine oil, and the firstlings of thy herds and of thy flocks; that thou mayest learn to fear the LORD thy God always."* (Deuteronomy 14:23) The tithe was never just about provision for the Levites; it was also about shaping the people. By setting apart their increase and bringing it to the Lord's chosen place, they learned to fear Him, to remember His ownership, and to rejoice in His blessing.

Do not miss the practical mercy at the edges of the design: *"At the end of three years thou shalt bring forth all the tithe of thine increase the same year, and shalt lay it up within thy gates: and the Levite… and the stranger, and the fatherless, and the widow, which are within thy gates, shall come, and shall eat and be satisfied."* (Deuteronomy 14:28-29) Even the poor were sustained by the tithe.[4] God's design ensured that His house was supplied, His servants were provided for, His people were trained in worship, and the needy were cared for.

Even the Levites Tithed

As mentioned earlier, even the Levites tithed. And that detail is not a throwaway line—it's a window into God's heart for His people. The command is explicit: *"Thus speak unto the Levites, and say unto them, When ye take of the children of Israel the tithes which I have given you from them for your inheritance, then ye shall offer up an heave offering of it for the LORD, even a tenth part of the tithe. And this your heave offering shall be reckoned unto you, as though it were the corn of the threshingfloor, and as the fulness of the winepress. Thus ye also shall offer an heave offering unto the LORD of all your tithes… and ye shall give thereof the LORD's heave offering to Aaron the priest."* (Numbers 18:26-28)

Two things are happening here. First, the Levites live from the people's tithe—God's design for sustaining temple service. Second, the Levites themselves must lift a tenth from what they receive and give it to the priests, *"of all the best*

---

[4] Regular tithes were centralized at the place God chose (Deuteronomy 12); in the third year, a local provision ensured the Levites and poor were supplied within the gates (Deuteronomy 14:28-29).

thereof, even the hallowed part thereof out of it." (Numbers 18:29) In other words, those who lived off the holy portion still had to treat that portion as holy. No one in the system was exempt from honoring the Lord. The tithe didn't terminate on the receivers; it passed through their hands and rose back to God.

That alone tells us the tithe is more than a budget tool. If this were merely about keeping the lights on in the tabernacle, it would make no sense for receivers to give from what they received. But the Lord required it—open-handed leaders modeling open-handed worship—because giving shapes the giver. It trains the heart to live before God, not to clutch what is convenient. *Heave offering* is the right picture: they lifted it up to the Lord. Even the Levites—whose daily work was ministry—had to feel the tug of parting with the "best thereof" and learn again that *the LORD is their inheritance* (see Deuteronomy 10:9; Deuteronomy 18:1-2).

There's a holy logic in Numbers 18 that keeps everyone humble. The people bring the tithe; the Levites receive it; the Levites tithe the tithe; and all of it is treated as if it were fresh from God's hand. No one is allowed to become a cul-de-sac. God builds a flow into the life of His house so that every hand—pew and pulpit—stays open. It guards the ministers from entitlement, it guards the people from stinginess, and it keeps the whole nation rehearsing the same confession: *"It is holy unto the LORD."* (Leviticus 27:30)

Think of the formation baked into that rhythm. The farmer learns it at the threshing floor. The Levite learns it at the storehouse. The priest learns it at the altar. All of them, in their station, act out the same truth: God owns it; we return the best; we live by what He provides. That is why this moment is so much bigger than "paying the clergy." Giving is as good for the giver as it is for the receiver. It acknowledges dependence, cultivates gratitude, and honors God—*especially* when the ones giving are the very ones serving in His name.

And notice the Lord's care for the tone of the whole thing: *"Of all your gifts ye shall offer every heave offering of the LORD, of all the best thereof, even the hallowed part thereof out of it."* (Numbers 18:29) Not leftovers, not the sweepings of the bin—the best. God's people, including God's servants, were to feel the worship in the weight of what left their hands. That is why I keep calling the tithe (and the offering) a thermometer. It doesn't set the temperature of the soul; it reveals it. And in Israel's life, God wanted *every* part of the body—leaders included—to read hot.

Bringing It Together

Under Moses we see the tithe defined as a tenth of all increase, holy to the Lord; directed to the place where God set His name and to the Levites who served in His house; and designed to sustain God's work while shaping God's people in reverent worship and joyful dependence. The pattern is unmistakable. The tithe did not fund luxuries; it underwrote the basic operation of worship. Priests could minister because the people were faithful. And even the Levites had to tithe, because the act itself was worship, not merely utility.

This is why the argument, "The tithe was just for Israel,"

will not hold. The principle is too deep, too broad, too worship-centered to be boxed into a single era. It is God's design for His people. Whether your increase is pears, beets, or a paycheck, the principle is the same: *"all the tithe… is the LORD's: it is holy unto the LORD."* (Leviticus 27:30)

CHAPTER FOUR

WHEN THE HOUSE IS SUPPLIED: HEZEKIAH, NEHEMIAH, AMOS, AND MALACHI

"Full storehouse, flourishing people; empty storehouse, withering hearts."

I can think of dozens of moments in my own life when I've watched God provide in ways I could never have orchestrated. And the common thread in all of them has been this: when I obeyed in giving—when I tithed faithfully and gave above and beyond with a joyful heart—God always made sure the needs were met, and more besides.

I'll never forget one story in particular. It was the year before I got married. Kailley was working two jobs to save up for wedding expenses. I was in law school, running an internet-based business on the side. Things were tight. I had just bought a house, bills were stacking up, and I had to figure out how to pay for books and tuition.

Then a missionary came through our church. I had $700 sitting in my checking account—saved for law school books. That was it. That was all I had. But both of us felt the Lord nudging us to give. So, nervously, we did. We gave the missionary the $700 and put the need for law school books into God's hands. It was the most nerve-wracking decision of our young lives.

One week later, I was in a car accident. Thankfully it was minor. But the insurance company not only paid off my car—they gave me a settlement check of over $20,000 for "pain and suffering." That more than paid for my books and covered a huge portion of law school expenses.

The second year of law school, the same thing happened. Tight finances, faithful giving, and then—another car accident, another settlement, another unexpected provision. By the third year I told the Lord I was a little nervous about praying too specifically! But the lesson was clear: you cannot out-give God. When you obey Him in tithing and giving, He opens the windows of heaven in ways you could never predict.

And that's exactly what we see in Scripture.

Hezekiah: Tithing Restored and Prosperity Returned

When King Hezekiah stepped onto the scene, Judah was spiritually bankrupt. His father Ahaz had shuttered the temple, snuffed out the lamps, and scattered the Levites. Hezekiah's first move was to swing the doors back open and call God's people to order—cleansing the house, re-consecrating the priests, restoring worship (2 Chronicles 29). Then he did something intensely practical: he reestablished God's supply line.

He set the example himself: *"Moreover he commanded the people that dwelt in Jerusalem to give the portion of the priests and the Levites, that they might be encouraged in the law of the LORD."* (2 Chronicles 31:4) Do you see the aim? Not payroll for its own sake—*encouragement in the law of the LORD*. When those who serve in the house are supplied, they can give themselves fully to teaching, intercession, and the holy things.

What happened next reads like revival in ledger form. *"As soon as the commandment came abroad, the children of Israel brought in abundance the firstfruits of corn, wine, and oil, and honey, and of all the increase of the field; and the tithe of all things brought they in abundantly."* (2 Chronicles 31:5) The chronicler slows down to show you the piles: *"In the third month they began to lay the foundation of the heaps, and finished them in the seventh month."* (2 Chronicles 31:7) Months of steady, joyful obedience—so much so that Hezekiah had to order storerooms to be prepared: *"Then Hezekiah commanded to prepare chambers in the house of the LORD; and they prepared them, and brought in the offerings and the tithes and the dedicated things faithfully."* (2 Chronicles 31:11-12)

I love the high priest's report when the king comes to see the heaps for himself. Azariah says, *"Since the people began to bring the offerings into the house of the LORD, we have had enough to eat, and have left plenty: for the LORD hath blessed his people; and that which is left is this great store."* (2 Chronicles 31:10) Enough—and plenty left. Not extravagance, not excess for luxury—sufficiency with overflow for the work.

Hezekiah also built accountability into the system. The text names the overseers who handled the tithes and distributions to the priests, Levites, and their families—men like Cononiah and Shimei—because integrity in God's house matters (2 Chronicles 31:12-19). This was not a free-for-all; it was faithful stewardship so that no one lacked and no ministry stalled.

And the verdict? Scripture ties a bow on the whole season: *"Thus did Hezekiah throughout all Judah, and wrought that which was good and right and truth before the LORD his God. And in every work that he began in the service of the house of God, and in the law, and in the commandments, to seek his God, he did it with all his heart, and prospered."* (2 Chronicles 31:20-21) When the tithe flows, the house is supplied; when the house is supplied, the Word runs; when the Word runs, the people flourish. That is not slot-machine theology; it is the ordinary grain of God's world—obedience leading to God-given sufficiency, with "plenty left" to keep the work strong.

Nehemiah: "We Will Not Forsake the House of Our God"

When Nehemiah arrived, Jerusalem's walls were rubble and the people's worship was threadbare. Covenant renewal began in earnest: public reading of the Law (Nehemiah 8), confession (Nehemiah 9), and a written pledge that included

this line of steel: *"And we will not forsake the house of our God."*
(Nehemiah 10:39) That pledge had teeth. They promised
firstfruits, wood for the altar, portions for the singers and
gatekeepers, and—crucially—the tithes into designated store
rooms so the Levites could minister without scrambling for a
living (Nehemiah 10:32-39; 12:44-47).

But turn the page to Nehemiah 13 and you feel the floor
drop. While Nehemiah was back in Persia, *"Eliashib the priest,
having the oversight of the chamber of the house of our God, was allied
unto Tobiah."* (Nehemiah 13:4) Tobiah—the longtime mocker
and enemy of the work (see Nehemiah 2:10, 19; 4:3)—was
given a suite *inside* the temple complex: *"he had prepared for him
a great chamber, where aforetime they laid the meat offerings, the
frankincense, and the vessels, and the tithes of the corn, the new wine,
and the oil."* (Nehemiah 13:5) Read that slowly. The very room
designed to hold God's portion had been emptied of tithes
and filled with an enemy's furniture.

Here is the principle in bold letters: if you do not fill
God's house with God's portion, something else will move
in. Sacred space never stays empty; it gets occupied—by
enemies, by ego, by lesser priorities.

Nehemiah returned, saw the desecration, and went holy-
wild. *"It grieved me sore: therefore I cast forth all the household stuff of
Tobiah out of the chamber."* (Nehemiah 13:8) He ordered the
rooms cleansed, restored the vessels, frankincense, and
offerings (Nehemiah 13:9), and then asked the piercing
question that echoes into every generation: *"Why is the house of
God forsaken?"* (Nehemiah 13:11)

Because the store rooms had been repurposed, the

supply line broke. The Levites and singers *"that did the work, were fled every one to his field."* (Nehemiah 13:10) No tithes, no ministers. No ministers, no ministry. Nehemiah gathered them back, *"set them in their place,"* and then did more than shout—he built structure. He *"made treasurers over the treasuries,"* naming trustworthy men—Shelemiah the priest, Zadok the scribe, Pedaiah of the Levites, with Hanan as assistant—*"for they were counted faithful,"* and he assigned them concrete responsibilities *"to distribute unto their brethren."* (Nehemiah 13:12-13) The result? *"Then brought all Judah the tithe of the corn and the new wine and the oil unto the treasuries."* (Nehemiah 13:12)

Two takeaways matter for us.

First, the Tobiah Test: when the tithe dries up, enemies don't just heckle from the wall—they haul in their furniture. In our day it may not be a man named Tobiah, but the principle stands. When God's portion is withheld, God's work is displaced. Ministries wither, shepherds scatter to the fields, and the chambers meant for prayer, Word, and mercy get crowded by whatever can pay the rent.

Second, zeal must be paired with stewardship. Nehemiah didn't only purge; he appointed. He matched repentance with processes, passion with accountability. He safeguarded the store rooms so the Levites could sing, teach, and serve without leaving their posts to survive.

Nehemiah ends that whole episode with a prayer that fits anyone who loves God's house: *"Remember me, O my God, concerning this... and spare me according to the greatness of thy mercy."* (Nehemiah 13:14, 22) In other words, "Lord, I threw Tobiah's couch into the street, I cleansed the rooms, I put your people back on duty, and I rebuilt the supply line—do not let your house be forsaken on my watch."

Neither should it be on ours.

Amos: Sarcasm and a Stinging Reminder

But tithing is never just about money. Amos makes that painfully clear. Israel was still "doing church"—pilgrimages, offerings, public displays of generosity—yet their lives were out of joint. So the prophet unsheathes holy sarcasm:

"Come to Bethel, and transgress; at Gilgal multiply transgression; and bring your sacrifices every morning, and your tithes after three years: and offer a sacrifice of thanksgiving with leaven, and proclaim and publish the free offerings: for this liketh you, O ye children of Israel, saith the Lord GOD." (Amos 4:4-5)

In other words: keep the donations rolling—if spectacle is what you love—but do not imagine that performance covers rebellion. God is not bribed by religious busyness. He goes further in the same book: *"Though ye offer me burnt offerings and your meat offerings, I will not accept them... Take thou away from me the noise of thy songs... But let judgment run down as waters, and righteousness as a mighty stream."* (Amos 5:22-24) The problem was not a lack of activity; it was a lack of integrity—cracked scales, crushed poor, hard hearts. *"Hear this, O ye that swallow up the needy... saying, When will the new moon be gone, that we may sell corn?... making the ephah small, and the shekel great, and falsifying the balances by deceit?"* (Amos 8:4-5)

Put simply: generosity without justice is noise. *Tithing without truth is theater.* The Lord wants a life that matches the gift. First Samuel says it this way: *"To obey is better than sacrifice."* (1 Samuel 15:22) Jesus will echo Amos straight across the centuries when He rebukes the Pharisees for tithing the spice rack and neglecting the "weightier matters" of *"judgment, mercy, and faith."* (Matthew 23:23)

So Amos stands as a warning and a mercy. A warning, because God rejects offerings brought with crooked scales and cold hearts. A mercy, because He tells us exactly what He does receive: repentant, obedient worship that flows into straight dealings, clean hands, open eyes for the poor, and a tithe that is the overflow of a right heart. When righteousness runs like a river, the gifts finally mean what they should.

Malachi: Robbing God or Receiving Blessing

Set the scene. Judah is back from exile. The temple stands, but hearts are shabby. Priests cut corners; worship limps. Into that weariness the Lord speaks with a thunderclap of immutability: *"For I am the LORD, I change not."* (Malachi 3:6) On the heels of that sentence—before four centuries of prophetic silence—He addresses their wallets:

"Will a man rob God? Yet ye have robbed me. But ye say, Wherein have we robbed thee? In tithes and offerings. Ye are cursed with a curse: for ye have robbed me, even this whole nation. Bring ye all the tithes into the storehouse, that there may be meat in mine house, and prove me now herewith… if I will not open you the windows of heaven, and pour you out a blessing…." (Malachi 3:8-10)

Notice the moral charge: *robbery.* God does not say, "You've been a little tight." He says, "You have taken what is mine." Notice the scope: *all the tithes*—no skimming, no partial compliance. Notice the destination: *the storehouse… that there may be meat in my house*—the Levites and temple service lack supply because the people have withheld the holy portion. And notice the dare: *"Prove me now."* Nowhere else does God invite His people to test Him by obedience in this way. The promise is multi-layered: *"open… the windows of heaven," "pour you out a blessing," "I will rebuke the devourer for your sakes,"* and *"all nations shall call you blessed."* (Malachi 3:10-12) In other words: supply for the house of God, protection against loss, and a public testimony of God's favor.

And do not miss the timing. The last prophetic word before the long hush of intertestamental silence is not a relaxation of the tithe but a rebuke for withholding it and a gracious invitation to return. If tithing were about to evaporate under grace, why would the Lord anchor it to His unchanging character and make it His parting charge?

Now, two clarifications keep us honest and balanced.

First, *Christ bore the curse of the Law for our salvation* (Galatians 3:13). That does not mean our Father no longer disciplines His children or that creation's grain no longer runs in God's moral order. The New Testament repeats Malachi's logic in different words: *"Be not deceived; God is not mocked: for whatsoever a man soweth, that shall he also reap."* (Galatians 6:7) Paul applies that to generosity: *"He which soweth sparingly shall reap also sparingly; and he which soweth bountifully shall reap also bountifully… and God is able to make all grace abound toward you… being enriched in every thing to all bountifulness."* (2 Corinthians 9:6-11) We are not "buying blessing." We are walking in the grain of God's world. Under grace, the calculus is not leverage but lordship.

Second, this is not prosperity slot-machine theology. Sometimes the "windows of heaven" look like abundance; sometimes like sufficiency, contentment, and protection from losses we never even saw circling (2 Corinthians 9:8; 1 Timothy 6:6-8). The point of Malachi is not a gimmick. It is God: *"I am the LORD, I change not."* He claims His portion, He loves His house, He trains His people, and He delights to bless obedience.

Take Malachi on his own terms, then watch how the New Testament resumes the same melody after the silence. Jesus will say, *"These ought ye to have done."* (Matthew 23:23) Paul will add, *"Even so hath the Lord ordained."* (1 Corinthians 9:14) Malachi is not an awkward relic to be explained away; it is the Spirit's last Old-Covenant word on a first-order issue: when God's house is supplied, God's work flourishes; when His portion is withheld, His people wither. The invitation still stands: *bring all the tithes… prove me now…* and watch the faithfulness of the God who does not change.

The Thread that Ties It Together

From Hezekiah's prosperity, to Nehemiah's reforms, to Amos' rebuke, to Malachi's promise, the message is consistent. When the tithe flows, God's house thrives and His people prosper. When the tithe is withheld, God's work falters and His people suffer. When the tithe is given without a right heart, God rejects it. When the tithe is given in faith and gratitude, God pours out blessing.

It's not about funding God as though He were broke. It's about obedience, gratitude, and worship. And take it from me—I've lived it—you cannot out-give God.

That's what Malachi promised. That's what I've seen. That's what Hezekiah and Nehemiah proved. And that's what God still does today.

CHAPTER FIVE

CHRIST'S AFFIRMATION

"If Christ affirmed it, why do we argue against it today?"

The word *tithe* is only used three times in the New Testament—and all three come directly from the mouth of Jesus. Two of those are parallel accounts (Matthew 23:23 and Luke 11:42), and the other is in a parable (Luke 18:12). That's it. Three mentions, two moments. But what Jesus does with those mentions is crucial.

"These Ought Ye to Have Done"

In Matthew 23:23 (repeated in Luke 11:42), Jesus confronts the Pharisees. Hypocrisy seems to have been their spiritual hobby. They were meticulous in outward obedience, tithing even on their spices—mint, anise, and cummin. They could calculate down to the leaf.

But Jesus wasn't impressed. Their hearts were rotten. They tithed, yes, but they neglected *"the weightier matters of the law, judgment, mercy, and faith."* It would be like a husband saying to his wife: *"Sure, I forgot your birthday, ignored our anniversary, yelled at you, and treated you with contempt—but I never committed adultery, so technically I kept the rules!"* What a sham.

That's the Pharisees. They dotted the "i's" and crossed the "t's" but missed the heart. Yet listen carefully to what Jesus says: *"These ought ye to have done, and not to leave the other undone."* (Matthew 23:23) This was spoken under the Mosaic economy, yet affirming a moral/creation-order principle that the cross intensifies, not erases.

Did you catch that? He doesn't condemn their tithing. He condemns their hearts. But in doing so, He reaffirms the tithe: *"these ought ye to have done."* If tithing were abolished under grace, that was His moment to say it. He could have cleared the slate, lifted the standard away, and said, "That was Old Covenant, no longer binding." Instead, He says the opposite.

Jesus affirms the practice and elevates the heart. He ties tithing to justice, mercy, and faith. He takes the Pharisees' hollow arithmetic and fills it with living substance. That alone should stop us in our tracks. If Christ had wanted to strike tithing from His people's obedience, this was His pulpit, His chance. But He did not. When Jesus affirms something before the cross, either (1) it belongs to the ceremonial system that His death fulfills and therefore passes (sacrifices, dietary codes, temple rites), or (2) it reflects moral/creation order that the cross intensifies and carries forward (marriage, truthfulness, stewardship, justice/mercy/faith).[5] His "these ought ye to have done" locates tithing with the latter—tied to worship and justice—while rejecting heartless legalism.

And here's something worth pondering. When does Jesus ever encourage less giving? I can't find a single instance.

He points to the widow who gave two mites—*all her living*—and says she gave more than everyone else (Luke 21:1-4). That's not ten percent. That's one hundred percent. He tells the rich young ruler, *"Sell all that thou hast, and distribute unto the poor, and thou shalt have treasure in heaven: and come, follow me."* (Luke 18:22) Not because selling possessions could earn salvation, but because full surrender reveals the heart.

Think about that. Jesus praises total sacrifice, points to radical generosity, and calls out empty religion—but He never once lowers the standard. Never once does He say, "Ten percent is too much, dial it back." If anything, He keeps raising the bar.

So what do we do with that? We stop treating the tithe as a tax and start seeing it as worship. Jesus never dismissed it, never mocked it, never minimized it. Instead, He folded it into the larger call: a heart full of justice, mercy, and faith, expressed in faithful, tangible giving.

---

[5] When distinguishing ceremonial law (fulfilled in Christ's death) from moral order (carried forward under grace), Scripture offers clear examples. Ceremonial practices such as animal sacrifices, priestly rituals, and dietary codes pass away (Hebrews 10:1-12; Mark 7:18-19; Colossians 2:16-17). But moral commands like marriage (Matthew 19:4-6), truthfulness (Matthew 5:37), and care for the poor (Matthew 19:21; Galatians 2:10) are reaffirmed and even intensified. Tithing fits this second category: a creation-order principle of stewardship and worship, not a temporary ceremonial code.

The Pharisees missed it because they thought math could replace mercy. But Jesus says both matter. *"These ought ye to have done, and not to leave the other undone."*

Fasting and Tithing Together

The third use of the word *tithe* comes in Luke 18:12, in Jesus' parable of the Pharisee and the publican. The Pharisee boasts: *"I fast twice in the week, I give tithes of all that I possess."*

Now remember—this isn't even a historical event Christ was commenting on. He created the story as a parable, crafted on purpose to teach us something eternal. He could have chosen any example of religious pride. He could have said, "I pray three times a day," or, "I keep the Sabbath perfectly." But He didn't. He deliberately put fasting and tithing together in the mouth of the Pharisee. Two disciplines that require faith, obedience, and sacrifice.

And here's what's striking: neither is abolished. Jesus does not dismiss fasting, and He does not dismiss tithing. Instead, He exposes the pride that poisoned both. The Pharisee's downfall wasn't that he tithed or fasted, but that he trusted in those acts to make him righteous. His pride condemned him, not his practice.

But step back and look at the pairing. Fasting and tithing. Both are costly. Both require denying yourself. Both are disciplines that feel hard in the flesh but bring strength in the Spirit. And both are tied to "big things" in the Christian life—fasting when you need breakthrough (Mark 9:29), and tithing when you want God's house supplied and His blessing poured out.

No one argues that fasting was abolished in the New Testament.[6] In fact, Jesus assumed His disciples would fast: *"When ye fast, be not, as the hypocrites, of a sad countenance."* (Matthew 6:16) Notice that—*when*, not *if.* Later He says, *"This kind can come forth by nothing, but by prayer and fasting."* (Mark 9:29) Fasting remains a living, breathing discipline of faith. So why would tithing—mentioned in the same breath— suddenly vanish? It doesn't.

Now, I can already hear the objection: "But wait—this was before the death of the Testator! Hebrews 9:16-17 says a testament is not in force until after men are dead. So Matthew 23:23 and Luke 18:12 don't apply to us in the church age—they're Old Testament, not New."

That's a fair observation to raise, but it doesn't hold. Yes, Jesus spoke these words before the cross. But here's the key: when He affirms something pre-cross, it falls into one of two categories. If it is part of the ceremonial law—sacrifices, dietary codes, temple rituals—then His death fulfills it and it passes away. But if it is part of God's moral order or His creation-level principles, then the cross doesn't abolish it—it carries it forward.

Jesus Himself showed this in the Sermon on the Mount.

---

[6] Like tithing, fasting is not ceremonial. It was practiced by Gentiles and regarded by God: Nineveh "proclaimed a fast" and "God saw their works" (Jonah 3:5–10); Darius, a Persian king, "passed the night fasting" for Daniel (Daniel 6:18). Its moral logic also appears in the likely pre-law setting of Job: *"I have esteemed the words of his mouth more than my necessary food."* (Job 23:12) In the New Testament, Christ assumes and regulates fasting— "when ye fast …" and "then shall they fast" (Matthew 6:16–18; Mark 2:20)—and the apostolic church practices it (Acts 13:2–3; 14:23; 1 Corinthians 7:5, Mark 9:29). Thus fasting—like the tithe given pre-law (Genesis 14:20; 28:22), honored beyond Israel, and reaffirmed by Christ— belongs to ongoing moral law, not a ceremonial shadow.

He didn't erase the moral law: *"Thou shalt not kill."* He raised the bar: *"Whosoever is angry with his brother without a cause shall be in danger of the judgment."* (Matthew 5:22) He didn't erase marriage; He reaffirmed it. He didn't erase stewardship; He heightened it. In the same way, He didn't erase tithing; He tied it to the heart.

Yes, Matthew 23:23 and Luke 18:12 are spoken before the death of the Testator. But instead of dismissing them, that timing clarifies the continuity. Jesus never lowers the bar.[7] He never once says, "Give less." If anything, He raises the standard—praising a widow who gave 100% and challenging a rich man to sell all.

The Pharisee's mistake was not that he tithed and fasted. It was that he trusted the act instead of the God behind it. And that's the same lesson for us: fasting and tithing don't justify us, but they do shape us. They keep our hearts humble, our hands open, and our worship pointed to the One who owns it all.

So where does that leave us? With a Saviour who never once lowered the bar of generosity. A Saviour who could have dismissed tithing in a single breath but instead affirmed it: *"These ought ye to have done."* A Saviour who crafted a parable where tithing and fasting stood side by side as disciplines of faith, obedience, and sacrifice. A Saviour who pointed to a

---

[7] Jesus consistently raised, not relaxed, the moral bar. For example, He deepened "Thou shalt not kill" into the heart-issue of anger (Matthew 5:21-22) and "Thou shalt not commit adultery" into the inward lust of the eyes (Matthew 5:27-28). He raised oaths into simple truthfulness (Matthew 5:33-37), retaliation into radical forgiveness (Matthew 5:38-39), and love for neighbors into love for enemies (Matthew 5:43-44). At every point He heightened obedience, never reduced it.

widow giving 100% and a rich man unwilling to part with anything—and made it clear that giving is always a matter of the heart.

If Christ Himself never encouraged less, why should we? The tithe is not a tax to escape. It is a testimony to embrace. It declares, "God owns it all, my heart trusts Him, and my hands are open." It shapes us, humbles us, and ties us to the living High Priest who still receives it.

That's why tithing isn't about legalism or loopholes. It's about lordship. It isn't about percentages on paper. It's about priorities in worship. And when the gospel grips our hearts, when gratitude wells up, ten percent no longer feels like a ceiling but a floor.

Christ could have silenced tithing. Instead, He sanctified it. And He calls us to give—not less, but more—because when glory and thanks are alive in our hearts, we stop asking, "How little can I give?" and start saying, "Lord, it's all Yours."

CHAPTER SIX

MORE THAN MONEY—BEYOND THE BASELINE

"Grace doesn't erase the tenth; it energizes it—and then pushes us past it with joy."

By the time we reach Paul's letters, Jesus has reaffirmed the tithe and the church in Acts is already running hot with generosity. Paul does not dismantle that foundation; he explains its rhythm, roots it in the Lord's own ordinance, and then lifts our eyes to grace that overflows the baseline.[8] In this chapter, we'll look at the rhythm (1 Corinthians 16), the right (1 Corinthians 9), and the overflow (2 Corinthians 8–9).

---

[8] By 'baseline' I mean a tithe (10% of increase) set apart to God for the life and work of your local church.

The Storehouse Rhythm in the Church

Paul's practical instruction to Corinth sounds familiar if you've been listening to Moses: a set time, a gathered people, a proportionate plan. *"Upon the first day of the week let every one of you lay by him in store, as God hath prospered him; that there be no gatherings when I come."* (1 Corinthians 16:2) Whether kept at hand or brought in weekly, Paul's point is no last-minute scramble—*"that there be no gatherings when I come."* It rides the first-day rhythm and as-prospered proportion—the same rails the church already used for ordinary support (tied to 1 Corinthians 9:14).

The *"first day"* marks the weekly rhythm of worship. *"Every one of you"* removes the idea that giving is for a special class. *"As God hath prospered"* keeps proportion at the heart of the practice. And *"in store"* places the collection within the life of the assembly so there's no last-minute scramble when needs surface.

Some note that 1 Corinthians 16 is addressing famine relief for Jerusalem, not the ordinary support of a congregation. True—and that's the point. When a special need arose, Paul didn't invent a brand-new mechanism. He ran the mercy gift down the same rails the church already used: the first-day rhythm, everyone participating, as-prospered proportion, gathered *"in store"* among the saints. Whether the money was kept at hand or placed weekly in the assembly, Paul's aim is clear: no panicked collections, just steady, thoughtful faithfulness. The famine gift rides a track that already exists.

And why does that track exist? Because the church is now the locus of God's gathered worship. Paul calls it *"the house of God, which is the church of the living God."* (1 Timothy 3:15) Under Moses, the storehouse was the temple where God set His name; under Christ, the "storehouse" reality is the local assembly where God dwells by His Spirit. Same Owner, new address. What follows is a principled, church-related application from 1 Timothy 3:15—not a 1:1 temple-to-church command. The principle continues: God's people bring God's portion into God's house for God's work.

"Even So": The Lord's Ordinance

Paul then gives the theological engine that pulls this train. *"Do ye not know that they which minister about holy things live of the things of the temple? … Even so hath the Lord ordained that they which preach the gospel should live of the gospel."* (1 Corinthians 9:13-14)[9]

"Even so" is the hinge. As surely as the Levites lived from the holy things, *even so* gospel ministers are to be supported by the giving of God's people. And note the weight: *"the Lord ordained."* This is not Paul's preference; it is Christ's appointment.

Paul anticipates the pushback and answers it in layers. First, common life teaches it: soldiers do not go to war at their own expense, farmers eat of their vineyards, shepherds

---

[9] Paul's "even so" parallels manner as well as right: those who served "lived from the temple… the altar," even so those who preach the gospel should live from the gospel. It's not merely permission to receive support; it points to the *ordinary way* that support happens.

drink the milk of the flock (1 Corinthians 9:7). Second, the Law teaches it: *"Thou shalt not muzzle the ox when he treadeth out the corn."* (Deuteronomy 25:4) Paul insists that command was written for our sake—laborers should share in the fruit of their labor (1 Corinthians 9:8-10). Third, simple equity teaches it: *"If we have sown unto you spiritual things, is it a great thing if we shall reap your carnal things?"* (1 Corinthians 9:11) Fourth, precedent teaches it: others received support at Corinth; how much more the apostle who planted them (1 Corinthians 9:12). Fifth, and finally, the temple pattern teaches it: *"they which minister about holy things live of the things of the temple."* (1 Corinthians 9:13)

Stack those arguments and the conclusion is inescapable: *"Even so hath the Lord ordained that they which preach the gospel should live of the gospel."* (1 Corinthians 9:14) The right to ministerial support is Christ-given. Paul sometimes waived that right for strategic reasons, working with his own hands so the gospel would not be hindered (1 Corinthians 9:12, 15). But his personal sacrifice does not erase the church's ordinary responsibility. A pastor may relinquish his claim; the people may not neglect their duty.

That is why the weekly "in store" of 1 Corinthians 16 and the *"even so"* of 1 Corinthians 9 belong together: one is the rhythm; the other is the rule. The rhythm keeps the house supplied; the rule explains why. In the temple economy Paul has in view, those who "*ministered about holy things"* were sustained by the tithe—that is how they *"lived of the things of the temple/ "* (Numbers 18) "Even so" signals not merely the *right* of support, but the ordinary means of that support under Christ: a sanctified tenth brought to God's house as His portion. The New Testament does not reprint the number, but the Lord's "even so" carries the pattern forward—support by the tithe as the baseline, with grace driving the overflow. Of course, the temple economy also included freewill offerings and other gifts; "even so" preserves that generosity while naming the ordinary backbone of ministerial support. The same pattern appears again when Paul cites Deuteronomy 25:4 to ground a creation-level ethic: *"The laborer is worthy of his reward."* (1 Timothy 5:17-18) Minister support isn't a temple artifact; it reflects God's enduring moral order.

Some readers will note the New Testament never reprints the word "tithe" as a direct command for Gentile believers. That's true—and worth saying plainly. But the New Testament often binds duties by pattern and ordinance rather than by repeating every Old Testament term. Here the pattern is weekly, proportionate, first-day giving gathered *"in store"* (1 Corinthians 16:2)—and yes, in context that collection was for relief, yet it still reveals the church's ordinary cadence of giving. The ordinance is the Lord's *"even so,"* which carries the temple's ordinary support of ministers into the church (1 Corinthians 9:13-14). Together they establish obligation without reprinting vocabulary. Jesus' *"these ought ye to have done"* keeps the floor from sinking (Matthew 23:23), while 2 Corinthians 8-9 lifts the ceiling with grace.

So I'm not arguing from silence; I'm arguing from continuity: (1) a pre-Law pattern (Genesis 14; Hebrews 7), (2) Christ's affirmation (Matthew 23:23), (3) an apostolic ordinance for ministerial support (1 Corinthians 9:14), and

(4) an apostolic rhythm for gathered giving (1 Corinthians 16:2). If a reader remains unconvinced, I gladly grant this: treat the tenth as the wise, time-tested floor that honors the same Owner and living Priest, then let grace run past it.

Unless the New Testament repeals the temple's ordinary means of ministerial support—or replaces it with a different ordinary means—the Lord's *"even so"* carries that provision forward. If someone believes the ordinary means has changed, it is fair to ask where Scripture teaches the repeal or the replacement.

Beyond the Baseline: Grace That Abounds

If 1 Corinthians supplies the mechanics and mandate, 2 Corinthians opens the heart. Paul points to the Macedonians: *"How that in a great trial of affliction the abundance of their joy and their deep poverty abounded unto the riches of their liberality."* (2 Corinthians 8:2) Afflicted, yet abounding. Poor, yet overflowing. Why? Because grace had seized them. *"For ye know the grace of our Lord Jesus Christ, that, though he was rich, yet for your sakes he became poor, that ye through his poverty might be rich."* (2 Corinthians 8:9)

Here is the New Testament shape of giving: the tithe remains the holy portion—the floor, not the ceiling—while grace drives the overflow. Paul refuses to fund the work by pressure or gimmicks. He reaches for worship. *"Every man according as he purposeth in his heart, so let him give; not grudgingly, or of necessity: for God loveth a cheerful giver."* (2 Corinthians 9:7) And he pairs worship with promise: *"He which soweth sparingly shall reap also sparingly; and he which soweth bountifully shall reap also bountifully… And God is able to make all grace abound toward you; that ye, always having all sufficiency in all things, may abound to every good work."* (2 Corinthians 9:6, 8) The outcome is practical as well as doxological: needs are met, thanksgiving multiplies, and God is glorified (2 Corinthians 9:11-12).

None of this suggests the tithe vanished. The earliest believers did not argue about whether to bring God's portion; they ran past it. Some sold land. Others laid gifts at the apostles' feet. In other words, offerings flowed beyond the baseline, but the baseline was still God's (see Acts 4-5). Grace does not abolish giving; grace amplifies it.

We see the same grace-overflow in Acts: believers sold lands and houses and *"laid them down at the apostles' feet"* for distribution (Acts 4:34-37; cf. Acts 2:44-45). The church also sent designated relief during famine, *"every man according to his ability,"* to the saints in Judea (Acts 11:27-30). Those gifts were extraordinary, need-driven offerings—not a replacement for the weekly, *"as God hath prospered"* rhythm (1 Corinthians 16:2), but the overflow of it. In other words, the *tithe funds the house; the Acts offerings fuel the surge.* In Acts, Luke doesn't frame these as abolishing the tithe but as extraordinary generosity that sprang from grace.

Parachurch, Missions, and the Storehouse First

What about missions agencies, relief funds, and ministries beyond the local church? Praise God for them. In the Old Testament, relief for the poor and feasts for rejoicing sat alongside the Levites' portion. In the New Testament, designated offerings speed relief and fuel mission. But the order matters. The tithe funds the house; the overflow fuels a thousand good works. Offerings can pass through parachurch hands; the point is not to replace the storehouse but to keep the storehouse first. Because pastors are charged with preaching the Word and oversight among a known flock, ordinary support is Biblically local, while extraordinary needs and missions are the joyful overflow.

Open Hands, Filled Hands

This is where Paul's theology meets our Tuesday morning. We give on the first day because the first day belongs to resurrection. We bring it "in store" because Christ has a household to feed and a mission to fund. We do it "as prospered" because God defines increase. We do it under *"even so hath the Lord ordained"* because it is His design, not ours. And then we keep going, because grace keeps going.

"Blessed be the Lord, who daily loadeth us with benefits, even the God of our salvation." (Psalm 68:19) He gives, we give, He gives more, we give more. Not to buy blessing, but to walk in His order. Not to impress Him, but to enjoy Him. Not about math, but about worship.

So let's name it plainly. The tithe is holy to the Lord— His portion, brought to His house, for His work. Paul keeps the storehouse rhythm and seals it with the Lord's ordinance. Then grace takes the baton and runs farther than percentages can measure. That is New Testament stewardship: a baseline of obedience, a spirit of joy, a life of open hands before the Lord of the tithe who still receives it.

A Final Thought: Why Argue Against the Baseline?

Every so often I read an article arguing that the tithe is a man-made invention of the early church, a fundraising mechanism the apostles never practiced. I don't want to ascribe motives; I'm sure most who write that way care about faithfulness. But I do want to ask a simple question: why advocate against the tithe? To what end?

Scripture is not shy here. Jesus says, *"These ought ye to have done."* (Matthew 23:23) Paul says, *"Even so hath the Lord ordained."* (1 Corinthians 9:14) Hebrews reminds us that our living High Priest still receives (Hebrews 7:8). The Bible repeatedly ties the Lord's portion to the Lord's house and the Lord's work. And when the New Testament showcases grace giving, it doesn't lower the floor; it raises the ceiling. Grace doesn't erase the tenth; grace energizes it—and then runs past it with joy.

So why spend precious ink to cast doubt on the baseline? I've watched what happens when God's portion dries up. Nehemiah did too. When the store rooms stood empty, Tobiah moved in. The enemy didn't merely sneer from the wall; he set up his furniture in the chamber meant for the tithes. The supply line broke, the Levites scattered, and worship withered (Nehemiah 13). If there is a Trojan horse in this conversation, it isn't the tithe sneaking legalism into grace; it's withholding sneaking drought into the work. Empty storehouses always find tenants.

And on the other side, I've watched what happens when believers treat the tenth as holy unto the Lord and then overflow into offerings: joy blooms, ministry strengthens, and God's people learn to trust Him. I am not preaching a prosperity gimmick. I am talking about the ordinary grain of God's world: obedience, then sufficiency; worship, then witness; the house supplied, then the Word running.

Sometimes the anti-tithe case leans on "history"—claims that the apostles didn't tithe and that percentage giving was formalized later. I'm not building this book on shifting secondary sources. Scripture is our final authority. The apostles' private budgets aren't recorded; their preaching is. Jesus' words are clear; Paul's ordinance is clear; the pattern is clear. When the Bible defines the tithe, the increase, the storehouse, and the purpose, we do not need to borrow authority from a footnote to erase what the text affirms.

And practically, why would we want to discourage a new believer from embracing a practice that so often jump-starts discipleship? Telling a young Christian, "Work your way up someday," can sound kind, but in practice it often robs them of the joy of obedience now. The tenth isn't a tax; it's a teacher. It trains the heart to put God first. Then grace takes over and giving grows. I've seen it. Many of you have too.

So my appeal is simple and gentle: err on the side of worship. If the Lord calls something holy, treat it as holy. If the apostles tie minister support to God's own ordinance, don't untie it. If Acts shows grace running beyond the baseline, don't move the baseline—run with grace. No harm comes to a church because her people honor God with the first tenth; much harm comes when the storehouse is empty and Tobiah finds a spare room.

I'm not trying to win an argument; I'm trying to protect a pipeline—God's portion to God's house for God's work—

and to invite you into the joy I keep talking about. The tithe won't save a soul and it won't fix a hard heart. But it will tell the truth about our trust, and it will keep the chambers filled so the song and the Word do not fall silent.

CHAPTER SEVEN

NUTS & BOLTS: HOW TO TITHE IN REAL LIFE

"God first, then the rest: practical tithing for real budgets."

Nothing here is tax, legal, or investment advice.

We've traced the tithe through the Old Testament, watched Jesus reaffirm it, and seen Paul carry it into the church. Now comes the practical question: how do we actually do this on Tuesday—when a paycheck hits, when a dividend posts, when a settlement check arrives, when business income is lumpy and strange?

Here's the model I've taught for years: keep it simple, keep it consistent, keep it obedient. If we hold those three together—and err on the generous side when the line is fuzzy—we'll do just fine.

Wages and Paychecks

Let's begin where it's simplest. You earn $1,000 this week. A tenth is $100. That's the tithe.

I teach gross, not net. Why? Firstfruits. God's portion comes off the top. The tax man doesn't outrank the Lord. Taxes are an expense of living in a society; they don't redefine what God calls "increase." Render to Caesar what is Caesar's—yes—but render to God what is God's, and God's comes first.

In everyday terms, "wages" means all the ways an employer pays you: salary, hourly pay, overtime, shift differential, tips, commissions, bonuses, holiday pay, PTO/vacation payouts, sick pay, hazard pay—if it shows up as pay on your stub, it's part of your increase. In the tax world we'd call this your gross income for wages: the pure, raw earnings before any adjustments or deductions. Most paychecks actually print it right there: Gross Pay at the top, then a list of withholdings.

Think of a paycheck in four lines:

1. **Gross pay** (what you earned).
2. **Pre-tax deductions** (401(k), HSA, FSA, some insurance).
3. **Taxes/withholdings** (federal, state, local, Social Security/Medicare).
4. **Net pay** (what lands in your account).

Firstfruits looks at line one. You tithe on what you earned, not what you cleared after everyone else took a bite.

If your employer withholds, the math is still easy: base your tithe on the gross number, not the net. And if you get a tax refund later, that's not new increase; it's simply your own money returning.

A few quick pictures:

1. **Salary.** Your contract says $5,200 for the month. Before withholdings, that's your increase. The tithe is $520.

2. **Hourly/overtime.** You worked 40 hours at $20 and 10 hours at time-and-a-half ($30). Gross is $1,100. The tithe is $110.

3. **Commission/bonus.** Your base check is $3,000 and your quarterly bonus is $2,000. Treat the bonus as the same kind of increase. Gross $5,000; tithe $500.

4. **Tips.** Whether they're reported on your stub or cash in your apron, tips are increase. Keep a simple running total and honor the Lord off the top.

5. **PTO/holiday pay.** Paid time off and holiday pay are still wages—tithe as usual.

6. **Severance.** Painful season, real increase. Tithe as the Lord provides and ask Him for the comfort that always travels with obedience.

If you make use of pre-tax savings (401(k), HSA, FSA), remember this: tithing on gross means you already honored the Lord on the dollars that went into those accounts. When you pull from them years later, you can tithe on the growth portion (I cover that later), but you don't need to "re-tithe" the same dollars twice.

For some of us, income doesn't land in neat, predictable amounts. Commissions come in bursts, tips rise and fall, and overtime shows up only when business demands it. The principle, though, stays the same: tithe ten percent of whatever you earn when you receive it, based on the gross. If your commission check is larger this month, tithe more; if your tips are smaller this week, tithe less. Whatever comes in, the tithe comes off the top. The simplest way to stay faithful is to set it aside immediately. Mark it in your budget, move it into a separate "firstfruits" account, or drop it in an envelope until Sunday. That way you're not scrambling later or tempted to spend what belongs to the Lord. The point is to make obedience the default: whenever God supplies increase, you return His portion right away. Keep it simple, keep it consistent, and you'll stay faithful.

Bottom line: if it increases your earnings as wages, it's part of your increase, and firstfruits means God gets His portion from the top—simply, consistently, obediently.

Business, Partnership, and Self-Employment Income

Now let's talk about the self-employed. This is where things can get messy, because revenue and profit are not the same thing. If you sell $10,000 worth of product on Amazon but spend $9,000 on goods, shipping, and fees, your real increase is $1,000. That's the amount you tithe on—$100 in that case.

But here's where people get into trouble: nickel-and-diming God with deductions. For tax purposes, you might write off part of your cell phone bill, mileage, or even your home office. But for tithing, I don't recommend shaving down your increase that way. If it's an expense you would've had regardless of the business—like the cell phone you were

NUTS & BOLTS: HOW TO TITHE IN REAL LIFE

already going to pay for—don't use it to shrink what you call profit. That shrinks generosity and muddies the spirit of firstfruits. Err on the side of giving, not squeezing.

And because profit ebbs and flows, you need a rhythm. Most small business owners aren't running a profit-and-loss statement every week—or even every month. So here's what I suggest: base your tithe on what you actually "pay" yourself from the business. If you transfer $2,000 from your business account to your personal account this month, tithe $200. Then, at the end of each quarter (or at year's end), reconcile against your actual profit and make up the difference. That way you're staying consistent without waiting until tax season to obey. And if a given period nets a loss, there's no increase to tithe; reconcile at quarter or year-end and give on true "profit."

One word of caution: keep your business and personal accounts separate. I've seen too many clients co-mingle funds—swiping the business debit card for groceries, vacations, or family expenses—and then claiming the business didn't "pay" them much. Suddenly, they say their tithe is $10 because $100 is all they technically "paid" themselves. That's neither simple nor generous; it confuses stewardship. Remember, the goal is to honor God, not to minimize Him.

And if your business is structured as a corporation or an S-corporation, the principle is clearer: the company is distinct from you. You tithe on what you personally earn—your wages, owner distributions, or dividends. Think of it like owning stock in Microsoft: you don't tithe on Microsoft's entire profit, you tithe when the dividend actually hits your account.

If you're a partner in a business, your increase shows up each year on the K-1. That number reflects your share of the profit, and profit is what Scripture calls increase. Even if the cash distribution lags behind, the income is still credited to you. Many believers find it most workable to tithe as actual cash distributions come in, then true-up at year's end once the books close and the K-1 tells the final story.

The bigger point is this: find a system that keeps your giving simple, consistent, and obedient. Don't let the complexity of business become an excuse for neglecting what belongs to God.

IRAs, 401(k)s, Pensions, and Other Retirement Accounts.

Retirement accounts create some of the most common tithing questions, and for good reason—they blend wages, tax law, employer benefits, and decades of growth into one pot. But the principle of increase still holds steady if we keep it simple, consistent, and obedient—settling fence questions with generosity.

Here's the way I explain it. If you contributed $100,000 into your 401(k) over the course of your working life, that $100,000 was your increase back then. If you tithed faithfully on your wages as they came in, then you've already honored the Lord with His portion on that money. What you see in retirement is a mix of that original $100,000 and whatever God allowed it to grow into. If the account is now worth $300,000, you could say that $200,000 is the increase.

Now, you don't need to track pennies of "basis versus growth" every time you make a withdrawal. That would overcomplicate what God designed to be simple. Instead, here's a straightforward way to handle it: when you draw money out, assume it's the increase first. In other words, if you withdraw $10,000, treat that $10,000 as profit for tithing purposes, not as though you're peeling back your old $100,000 contributions. It's not about clever accounting; it's about a generous posture that keeps God first. And if you tithed on gross during the earning years, you don't have to re-tithe those same dollars; my practice of treating withdrawals as 'gain first' is a generosity choice I personally make, not a rule.

This principle applies across the board. IRAs, 401(k)s, pensions, annuities, SEP-IRAs, or even military retirement pay—the question is always the same: is this increase in my hands right now? If so, tithe on it. If what you're receiving is truly just a return of something you already tithed on (rare, but possible with certain employer-funded pensions or unique plan structures), then the focus is on the growth portion.

The key in all of this is clarity and consistency. Pick a method you can explain with a clean conscience before God and stick with it. Don't hop back and forth depending on which angle saves you more. Remember, retirement accounts are not loopholes to avoid putting God first. They're simply another place where obedience shows up. And when the line gets gray, fall back on generosity. Even in retirement, our giving declares: "Lord, You are my provider. What I have is Yours."

Social Security and Disability

Here's how I handle Social Security (programs will vary but apply the same principle where you live – if benefits function as fresh provision, treat them as increase), and why. I don't treat those payroll withholdings as a personal investment that I'm later "getting back." They function more like a tax that funds a government program, not a savings account with my name on it. How do I know? My mother-in-law paid in for years, began receiving benefits at sixty-two, and then went to heaven not long after. There was no IRA-style payout of her "balance." That experience clarified it for me: Social Security contributions behave like taxes; the monthly benefit behaves like fresh income. On that understanding, when the checks start coming, I will tithe on them—not because I'm spoiling for an argument, but because I want to err on the side of firstfruits and keep my heart generous.

That said, I'm not trying to bind anyone's conscience with my story. If someone has tithed on gross wages all along and views the benefit as already tithed in principle, I won't fight them. But given how the system actually works, I treat the benefit itself as increase and gladly return the first tenth to the Lord. Generosity beats precision here, and peace of conscience is worth more than a clever spreadsheet.

Other Common Everyday Scenarios

I meet these questions all the time. The pattern underneath them is the same: if it enlarges your resources, it's increase; if it only replaces what you already had, it's not.

Health plans and HSAs. Keep the same first–fruits lens we've used all along: *increase* is money (or cash-equivalent value) that actually comes into your hand to direct. If funds become yours to steward, I treat them as increase and tithe when they arrive. If someone pays a bill upstream and no money ever becomes mine, that's not my increase.

Apply that to insurance premiums. When an employer pays my health-insurance premium straight to the insurer, no cash ever passes into my control. I'm grateful, but I don't count that as increase any more than I would a discount at the register. If, however, my employer gives me a taxable stipend or adds cash to my paycheck so I can buy coverage, that money *is* in my hand. I tithe on it when it's paid, then I pay the premium.

Health savings and spending accounts follow the same rule. Employer HSA deposits go into an account I own and control; that's fresh increase, so I tithe when it hits. My own HSA or FSA salary reductions were already tithed when I earned those wages; later reimbursements simply replace an expense, not create new increase. Most HRAs are employer-owned arrangements that only reimburse actual medical bills; because I never own unrestricted funds in an HRA, I don't treat those reimbursements as increase. If any plan functions like a cash allowance I control—some "health stipends" do—that's income in my hand, and I tithe on it. Tax treatment may differ, but our lens isn't the tax code; it's stewardship. If funds become yours to direct, that's increase.

The same logic settles the "what if someone pays my bill?" question. If a friend hands me $500 to help with surgery, that cash became mine to steward—I tithe on it, then pay the bill. If that friend pays the hospital directly, no funds ever passed through my hand; I don't count it as increase. Simple, obedient, consistent—and when a situation sits in the gray, I lean generous. I'd rather return a little extra of what was never really mine than whittle down the Lord's portion with clever categories.

Investments. With investments, the principle is simple: tithe on the gain. If you put in $10,000 and later sell for $15,000, the $5,000 increase is your titheable portion. That's straightforward enough when you're holding assets over time—real estate, a mutual fund, a stock position that matures.

But what about active accounts—day trading, frequent stock flips, or options contracts that swing wildly? Here's where simplicity keeps you sane. Imagine you deposit $50,000 into a brokerage account. One stock pops, and overnight your account balance jumps to $60,000. You sell, buy another stock, and before long the balance falls to $40,000. Nothing ever left the account. If you tithed on every trade, you'd not only be tangled in endless recordkeeping, you'd also be tithing on money you never truly gained—you actually lost. That's not the spirit of firstfruits; that's IRS-style math.

So here's the model I follow and commend: treat the account itself as a bucket. Gains inside the bucket rise and fall; they aren't "increase" until you actually draw from them. When you withdraw—whether to move funds to your checking account or to spend them—that's when you reckon increase. And here's where generosity guards the heart: I always assume the portion I'm withdrawing is gain before it is principal. If I put in $50,000, watch it grow to $60,000, and then take out $10,000, I don't tell myself, "Well, that's just part of my original." I treat it as increase and tithe on it. That posture keeps me from nickel-and-diming God while still honoring the principle of true increase.

The principle never changes: if it enlarges your resources, tithe on it. If it's just paper movement with no realized increase, you don't. Keep it simple. Keep it consistent. Keep it obedient. And when in doubt, lean generous.

Real estate. Rental income (including Airbnb and short-term rentals) is increase, plain and simple. Just as the self-employed tithe on their business profit, the landlord tithes on rental profit. The principle is the same: income minus legitimate expenses leaves you with increase. If you collect $1,200 in rent and spend $200 repairing a water heater, the $1,000 that remains is your increase, and the tithe belongs to the Lord on that amount.

But here's the caution: don't shrink God's portion by treating the IRS tax code as your tithe guide. On a tax return you can deduct things like depreciation, mileage to the property, or a home office. Those deductions make sense for tax purposes, but they don't always reflect actual out-of-pocket costs. Depreciation, for example, lowers your taxable income but doesn't shrink your bank balance. For tithing, I encourage landlords to keep it simple: subtract legitimate, unavoidable property expenses like repairs, utilities (if you pay them), property management fees, or insurance. What remains is increase. Don't nickel-and-dime God with technicalities. Err on the side of generosity.

Another way to make this manageable is to set a rhythm. Rental income can be steady, but expenses are often lumpy—one month you may have no repairs, the next month you're replacing a furnace. A good practice is to tithe on the net income as you collect rent, while keeping a running record of property expenses. Then, reconcile periodically—quarterly or annually—to make sure your tithe reflects your true profit. This keeps you consistent without getting paralyzed every time a tenant calls about a leaky faucet.

When it comes to selling a property, the same principle applies: tithe on the profit. If you bought a house for $200,000, invested $20,000 in genuine capital improvements, and later sold it for $260,000 after paying realtor fees and closing costs, your increase is $40,000. That's the portion you tithe on. If, after all costs, you simply break even, there's no increase to tithe.

Rental real estate really is no different than any other business. Keep the principle of increase in front of you, keep your system simple, consistent, and obedient, and when in doubt, lean toward generosity. God honors the heart more than the spreadsheets.

Windfalls, inheritances, gifts. Few moments test our heart toward increase like sudden windfalls. An inheritance, for example, enlarges your resources in one stroke. Whether it's land, money, or other assets, you now possess something you did not have before. That is increase, and it calls for firstfruits. Some believers stumble here because it feels like "free money," but that's the very reason it's a test: will I acknowledge the Lord even in this unexpected blessing? The same principle applies to gifts. If someone gives you cash, you've increased. It doesn't matter if it's $20 tucked in a birthday card or $2,000 slipped in an envelope—God has entrusted you with more than you had yesterday. Teach your children this while they are young.

Garage sales and used items. What about selling off old things? If you sell your bike for $100 when you originally paid $200, that's not increase. You already tithed when you earned the money to buy it. You've simply converted value from one form (a bike) back into another (cash). But let's say you sell something for more than you paid—maybe you bought a collectible for $50 and later sell it for $300. That $250 gain is increase, and it should be tithed. Simplicity keeps you from overcomplicating, and generosity keeps you from excusing yourself from giving when God has blessed you.

Insurance checks and settlements. Insurance is designed to make you whole, not wealthy. If your car is damaged in an accident and the body shop check pays for the repair, no increase has entered your hand. The same is true for a roof claim or a health reimbursement—those payments are replacements, not increase. But if a settlement goes beyond replacement—for example, money for "pain and suffering" or a lump-sum payout that exceeds actual loss—that surplus is increase. And increase is titheable. I know this personally. During law school, Kailley and I gave away the money we had saved for books, trusting the Lord. Shortly afterward, two settlement checks arrived—completely unexpected, perfectly timed. We tithed on them, and the Lord carried us through. To this day, I smile when I remember it. The checks weren't just provision; they were reminders that God Himself pays attention when we trust Him.

Scholarships and grants. Not every scholarship or grant counts as increase. If the funds are restricted—say, a scholarship that can only be paid directly to your college for tuition—you never actually have that money in your hand. It simply passes through, reducing a bill you would otherwise owe. That's relief, not increase. But if the scholarship or grant is broad-use—money that lands in your account and you can spend however you wish—then it enlarges your ability, and the principle of increase applies. Treat it as titheable income, and do it with thanksgiving that God has provided for your education.

Cash tips and side gigs. This one trips people up because so much of it is informal. Waiters, baristas, delivery drivers, weekend photographers, lawn-care helpers—tips and cash gigs feel small and irregular. But if it hits your hand as pay, it's increase. The IRS may not notice a $40 cash tip, but

God does. Don't wait until tax time or until you get a 1099 to decide whether it counts. Tithe as it comes in, then reconcile at the end of the year if you realize you under- or over-tithed. This keeps your heart soft and your obedience steady. Firstfruits doesn't wait on paperwork.

Gift cards and store credit. A gift card you can spend like cash is increase. If someone hands you a $100 Amazon card, you just gained the ability to buy $100 of value you didn't have before. That's increase, and I treat it as titheable. Whether you set aside the tithe when you receive it or when you actually use it is up to you—simplicity is the goal. Store credit from a return is different. That's just a swap: you gave merchandise back and got equivalent value to replace it. No new increase came into your hand.

Employer perks and bonuses. Employers get creative with compensation. Signing bonuses, retention bonuses, relocation stipends, or per-diem payments you keep beyond actual expenses—all of those enlarge your resources, so the principle is the same: tithe on them. But pure reimbursements for meals, mileage, or travel you already paid out of pocket don't count as increase; they're just repayment. If a benefit arrives as cash or a cash-equivalent you control (taxable stipend, allowance), treat it as increase; if it's a pure employer-paid bill with no cash in your hand, it's effectively a discount. The distinction comes back to increase: if you come out ahead, tithe; if it just makes you whole, you don't.

Unemployment and severance. Unemployment

benefits and severance checks are often overlooked in the middle of crisis, but they are still increase. They sustain you in a lean season, and that's precisely when firstfruits matter most. Keeping the tithe rhythm even in the valley is a declaration of trust: "Lord, You are my source, not this check." It may feel hard when the numbers are small, but consistency here is powerful. Remember Elijah and the widow of Zarephath: God honored her obedience in a time of drought.

Debt forgiveness and write-offs. Debt forgiveness sits in a gray area, but the guiding principles keep us steady. When a lender cancels a balance, your position improves, but that doesn't always mean you've "increased." If nothing new comes into your hands, you don't suddenly owe a tithe. Take mortgage relief programs as an example. Suppose you bought your home for $100,000 with a $100,000 mortgage, and the government steps in and forgives $30,000 of that debt. You don't tithe $3,000 that week. Nothing new came into your wallet; your obligation simply dropped. That's relief, not increase.

But here's where consistency comes in. If you later sell that same house for $100,000, your true cost wasn't $100,000 anymore—it was $70,000 after the relief. The $30,000 difference shows up as profit at the point of sale. That's genuine increase. That's when the principle of tithing applies.

The key is to distinguish between debt relief that lowers what you owe (which is a blessing, but not income), and forgiveness that leaves you holding resources free and clear (like cash in hand from a canceled loan). The former is relief;

the latter is increase.

And here's the safeguard against falling into the "net pay" argument. Tithing on gross wages is consistent because those dollars are truly yours the moment you earn them, even if the government snatches some for taxes before you see them. That's increase you controlled. Mortgage relief, on the other hand, isn't cash flow you controlled or spent—it's simply a lighter load on your shoulders until, later, it converts into actual increase when you sell.

The pattern holds: tithe on increase, not just improvement. Relief isn't income, but when relief produces tangible gain, that's the moment you bring the Lord's portion.

Credit-card rewards and cash back. Credit-card rewards are one of those modern wrinkles that force us to slow down and apply the principles. Most points and miles function like coupons or discounts—they reduce what you spent rather than add to what you have. If your grocery store gives you a $5 coupon at checkout, you wouldn't call that "increase"; it's just a discount. In the same way, if you swipe your card and earn 1% back in points that apply to your bill, that's not new income—it's simply a rebate on what you already purchased. Simplicity tells us not to overcomplicate this.

But sometimes those rewards pile up in ways that feel less like a coupon and more like cash. Cash-back that lands directly in your bank account enlarges your resources in the same way a dividend would—that's increase. And if your points accumulate to the point where you can buy something substantial—say, a $900 freezer for the basement that costs you nothing out of pocket—it starts to look and feel like fresh provision. That's where the principle of generosity comes in. Technically, you could treat it as a discount, but many times I'll choose to tithe on it, not because I "owe" it, but because I want my giving to mirror my gratitude. That's what I did with that freezer.

The principle is consistent: if it truly enlarges your resources, treat it as increase; if it merely discounts a purchase you've already tithed on, keep it simple and move on. And in the gray lines, lean generous. Better to err on the side of worship than to explain away God's blessing as a technicality.

Bank interest, bond coupons, royalties, and licensing. Some increase trickles in quietly. A few dollars of interest hitting your checking account each month, a bond coupon paying out twice a year, or a royalty check showing up in the mailbox. However it arrives, it's still increase. Small or large, those credits enlarge your resources, and the principle doesn't change: tithe on them.

Think about it: interest is money your money earned. It wasn't there before, now it is. That's the very definition of increase. Bond coupons work the same way—fixed payments in exchange for lending your capital. When they arrive, they enlarge your resources, so treat them as titheable income.

Royalties and licenses are often the most vivid examples. Maybe you wrote a book, recorded a song, designed a piece of software, or created a product under license. The checks that show up are what I call "seed-while-you-sleep" income.

You did the work once, and the fruit keeps coming in. Those payments are as much increase as a wage or a commission, even if they arrive on an irregular schedule. Tithe as the payments arrive, keeping the rhythm simple and consistent.

And here's where generosity can shape your posture. If your bank interest adds up to only a few dollars, it might feel negligible. But it's not about the math; it's about the worship. Honoring God with those small credits cultivates the same heart that will honor Him when the amounts are larger. Whether it's a trickle or a flood, the principle is the same: increase is increase, and the firstfruits belong to the Lord.

Crypto and digital assets. The digital economy has created new streams of income that didn't exist a generation ago—staking rewards, mining proceeds, airdrops, and trading gains. But the principle of tithing hasn't changed: increase is increase.

If you earn staking rewards or mining proceeds, those rewards enlarge your holdings the moment they hit your wallet. That's increase. The simplest and most consistent approach is to recognize their fair market value at the time you receive them and tithe on that value. Airdrops follow the same principle. When free tokens show up, they aren't monopoly money—they're new resources God has allowed into your hand. Treat them as increase.

Trading gains operate by the same rules as any other investment. If you buy at $1,000 and later sell at $3,000, the $2,000 gain is increase. Tithe on the gain, not the original capital. And for those who day-trade or churn assets frequently, simplicity is your friend. Don't try to tithe on every in-and-out. If your account is highly active, a workable rhythm is to tithe when you realize gains by pulling money out, always assuming what you withdraw represents profit first. This keeps obedience consistent without turning tithing into a bookkeeping nightmare.

And here's where generosity comes in. Some gray lines remain—what if you receive tokens that swing wildly in value before you can act? My counsel: pick a principle and stick to it, then err on the side of giving rather than withholding. God isn't impressed with perfect spreadsheets; He delights in faithful, worshipful hearts.

Crypto is new. The tithe is ancient. But the principle still holds: when your holdings enlarge, you acknowledge the Lord of the increase. Whether it's a paycheck, a dividend, or a digital token, the question is the same: will you honor Him with the firstfruits?

Employee stock and retirement matches. When your company contributes to your future through a 401(k) match, stock grants, or an Employee Stock Purchase Plan (ESPP), it's still compensation. The difference is timing and access. If the benefit is locked up until you vest or sell, then treat it like a delayed paycheck. You can cover it one of two ways: (1) tithe now by including it in your gross wages or (2) tithe later when the benefit actually vests, becomes yours, or you sell and realize the gain.

What matters most is not the timing but the principle: be consistent and keep it generous. With ESPPs or stock discounts, think of it like any other increase: if you bought shares for $8,000 that are immediately worth $10,000, the

$2,000 advantage is real gain, and it's appropriate to treat that as titheable when you take ownership.

I sometimes put it this way for simplicity: if you could cash it out today, it's increase; if you can't, then tithe when you can. Either way, don't nickel-and-dime God. The match or discount is a blessing. Build a rhythm that acknowledges it as His, and let generosity settle any gray areas.

Child support and alimony. These two categories often raise practical questions because they sit in unique places. Alimony received is straightforward: it comes into your hands as support for you, and it enlarges your household resources. For that reason, many believers treat alimony just like wages or any other form of income and tithe on it. It's not repayment of money you already tithed on; it's fresh provision in your account.

Child support, however, is more nuanced. The purpose of child support is to provide for the child's needs—food, clothing, school costs, medical expenses. In that sense, some believers treat it as a pass-through: money earmarked for the child rather than true increase for the parent. Others, however, still tithe on it as part of the household's overall increase, reasoning that every dollar flowing through their care should first honor the Lord. Whichever way you settle it, make sure the child's needs remain fully funded.

Here's where the principles of simplicity, consistency, and obedience come into play. If you view child support as a designated pass-through, then use it faithfully for your child without feeling guilty about not tithing directly on it. But if your conviction leans toward treating it as household increase, then tithe on it and trust the Lord to supply your child's needs through the ninety percent.

The key is not to waffle back and forth depending on the month's bills. Set a conviction before the Lord and walk in it consistently. Remember: the goal is not to trim it to the last cent in every scenario, but to keep your heart generous and your worship sincere. Whether it's alimony, child support, or any other form of provision, the principle remains the same: God gets first place in what He places in your hand.

Wedding gifts and GoFundMe. Few moments in life bring an outpouring of generosity like a wedding. Friends and family slip cards into your hand, envelopes pile up on the gift table, and you may leave the reception with more cash than you've ever held at once. Or perhaps it's not a wedding, but a season of need—your church takes up a love-offering for you, or a GoFundMe page is set up to help with unexpected expenses. However it comes, those funds enlarge your resources. They are increase. The principle applies the same way it would to wages or bonuses: set apart the Lord's portion first.

I often encourage couples to make their very first financial act as husband and wife an act of worship. Before the honeymoon, before the house, before anything else—sit down with those wedding envelopes, total them, and tithe together. It's a beautiful way to begin marriage with God first in your finances. The same goes for love-offerings or personal fundraising campaigns. If the money is given directly to you, not simply routed through you, it has enlarged your household's ability. Treat it as increase.

Now, there are times when funds may pass through your hands without belonging to you. Maybe someone uses your GoFundMe account to funnel support to a missionary friend, or perhaps your church entrusted you with money to deliver to another family. In those cases, you are only a channel, not a recipient. Passing money along for someone else is not your increase; it's their provision. The key is stewardship: move it along promptly, and don't confuse entrusted funds with personal blessing.

The principle here is clarity and honesty before God. If a gift or offering was meant for you, it's increase and should be tithed on. If it was meant for someone else and you're only the middleman, then it's not your increase at all. When in doubt, lean toward generosity. Better to give thanks with open hands than to slice the line so fine that worship gets lost in technicalities.

Jury duty, honoraria, and love-offerings. These come in many shapes and sizes, but the principle is the same: if it lands in your hand as pay, it's increase. A jury summons may feel like an interruption to your week, but the small check the county clerk hands you is still compensation for your service. A speaking honorarium, whether from a church pulpit, a conference stage, or a college lecture, is likewise income. The same goes for pulpit-supply gifts or the quiet "thank you" envelope pressed into your palm after filling in for another preacher. None of these payments are wages in the normal sense, but all enlarge your resources.

I've had people ask, "But isn't a love-offering different? Isn't that just a token gift?" Yes and no. The heart behind it may be different—it's given as gratitude, not as a wage contract—but the effect is the same: you have more in your hand than you did before. The increase principle still applies. If the Lord provides through the love of His people, then the tithe is still holy unto Him. Treat it like any other form of income.

This category is also where consistency guards against confusion. Don't get lost in trying to split hairs between a "stipend," an "offering," or an "honorarium." Whether it's $20 for jury duty, $200 for a wedding sermon, or $2,000 for a conference keynote, the principle doesn't change. Simplicity, obedience, and generosity will carry you through. Set aside the Lord's portion and receive the rest with thanksgiving.

And here's the joy: these unexpected gifts often feel like "extra"—above your ordinary paycheck or salary. That means tithing on them can feel especially sweet. It becomes less about calculation and more about celebration, another chance to say with your dollars what you're already saying with your lips: "Lord, all I have is Thine."

Final Thoughts

Let me land the plane on this "nuts & bolts" chapter by pulling the practical threads tight—and answering the Tuesday questions that tend to surface once the spreadsheets close and the heart work begins.

One Flesh, One Stewardship. First, in marriage, money is not "yours and mine"; it's ours. One flesh means one stewardship. Whether paychecks hit one account or two, we treat the household's increase as a single trust from God. We pray together, choose the same method together—gross or net, timing, reconciliations—and then we stay unified and consistent. If your spouse isn't yet on the same page, aim for conscience and unity more than victory. Start with what you can both do in faith, keep the tone gentle, and let your own faithfulness be a quiet message. Unity is part of the offering, even as each of us personally obeys the Lord.

Firstfruits Is a Posture. Firstfruits is a posture as much as a percentage. If you can, let your giving flow in the same rhythm as your income—weekly, biweekly, monthly—so obedience is automated and worship stays alive. We are not calculating a fee to keep God off our back; we are returning what is holy. The real danger is not over-giving, but turning the Lord into the IRS and hunting for loopholes. He is not a tax collector. He is our Father.

Teach this rhythm at home. When our kids were little, we used three boxes: God, Savings, Fun. Every birthday bill, every chore dollar, every odd-job envelope—first to God, then to future, then to fries. On Sundays they carried their money from the "God box" to church with a smile. As they grew, the boxes became a checking account, but the order never changed. Firstfruits became normal, not novel. That's what you want—not a debate every payday, but a default of worship.

When the Numbers Are Tight. "What if the numbers are tight?" Tight numbers don't erase the tithe; absence of increase, however, does. If there is truly no increase—job loss, zero income, a severe valley—you cannot tithe what does not exist. In famine, honor Him first with the little you do receive and seek wise counsel. He disciplines sons; He does not crush them. Debt raises similar questions. Paying down past foolishness is wise, but it does not come before honoring the Lord with present increase. Put Him first, then work your plan. You'll be surprised how often obedience creates room for progress.

If You're Behind. "What if I've missed past tithes—do I make them up?" You don't owe God back-taxes as if He were a creditor. But if your conscience is pricked, make a simple, joyful plan to set things right—add a percentage for a season, or dedicate a special gift when God provides. Do it as worship, not as penance. Grace doesn't keep score, but grace does move us to honor the Lord.

Gifts That Aren't Cash. "What if generosity shows up in ways that aren't cash?" The same principles still steer us. If you receive ownership or cash-equivalent value you control, that's increase. If you only receive the use of something— free rent for a semester, a borrowed car for a few months— thank God loudly and don't force it into a math problem. Simplicity keeps you honest; generosity keeps you warm.

Even Shepherds Bring Firstfruits. And yes, even pastors tithe. In Numbers chapter 18 the Lord required the Levites to tithe on the tithes they received. That was not bookkeeping; it was discipleship. No one in God's house stands above worship—not the offerer at the gate, not the singer on the platform, not the priest at the altar. In the same way, pastors and church staff should model what they teach. Shepherds who "live of the gospel" still honor the Lord of the tithe; bringing firstfruits keeps leaders humble and congregations healthy.

Some worry that a pastor tithing to the same church feels circular—"isn't that just money going out and coming back?" But the act is not a closed financial loop; it is an open-handed confession. The tithe is not a tip to a payroll; it is holy unto the Lord. A pastor's gift is offered to God through the storehouse like any other member's, without strings, designations, or self-benefit in view. He gives as a worshiper before he serves as a worker. That posture protects his own heart and strengthens the church's trust.

Practically, pastors can keep the same firstfruits rhythm they call the church to keep. Salary, housing allowance, love-offerings, and honoraria are increase and should be tithed as they are received. True reimbursements for ministry expenses are not increase. And for integrity's sake, it is wise for a church's finance team or treasurer to handle compensation and giving records—leaders should model generosity without managing who gave what. Clear lanes—elders set compensation, the treasurer counts the offerings, the pastor brings his firstfruits—make it easy for everyone to see that worship, not wiring, is what drives the moment.

When shepherds lead in giving, they quietly teach the flock how to walk. It says, "We are all under the same Lord. We all live by the same Book. We all bring the first and the best to God." That example is worth more than a dozen sermons. It keeps the minister low before God, the ministry supplied for the work, and the whole church reminded that the Owner of all still receives what His people return.

Wrapping It Up

So here's where we end up. Keep it simple: increase is increase. Keep it consistent: make it a rhythm, not a negotiation. Keep it obedient: firstfruits with a glad heart. Over all of it, keep the worship generous. With every gift we are saying, "Lord, Thou art greater. All I have is Thine. I joyfully return what is holy unto Thee." That is why I keep calling the tithe a thermometer. It doesn't heal a sick heart, but it does tell the truth about one. When the numbers line up with firstfruits, something healthy is happening inside. When they don't, the Spirit is inviting us back to trust.

So take the next paycheck, the next invoice, the next deposit—and put God first. Not about math. About glory and thanks. And watch how often the Father meets firstfruits with *"enough to eat, and… left plenty."* (2 Chronicles 31:10)

CHAPTER EIGHT

ANSWERING THE TOP 15 OBJECTIONS

"Honest questions. Clear Scripture. A steady path."

Talking about the tithe can stir a lot of feelings. Some of us carry good questions; some carry bad experiences; some just feel uncertain about what God actually asks of us. I understand. My aim in this chapter isn't to scold or win an argument—it's to help. If we're going to be Bible people, we have to let the Bible define its own terms. Scripture tells us what *"increase"* is, what the tithe is, where it goes, when it's brought, and—most importantly—whose it is: *"The tithe is the LORD's: it is holy unto the LORD."* (Leviticus 27:30)

That one sentence sets the tone. God owns it all. He has kept a holy portion for Himself. Our part is not to renegotiate, but to respond in faith. This isn't about

89

fundraising or pressure; it's about worship and trust. If the Lord calls something holy, the wisest, safest place for our hearts is to treat it as holy.

So here's how we'll proceed. We'll take the fifteen objections I hear most and walk them, gently and plainly, through Scripture. No arm-twisting, no guilt trips, no clever math—just open Bibles, clear reasoning, and a prayerful posture that says, "Speak, Lord." If your conscience is tender, I hope you find clarity and courage. If you're still sorting things out, I hope you find peace and a path you can walk with a clean heart before God.

In the end, the question isn't "Can I find an exception?" but "Will I honor Him?" Objections may be many, but truth is steady. Let's set the questions on the table, answer them carefully, and let God's Word have the last word.

1. "Tithing Was Just for Israel Under the Law."

This is one of the most common objections, and it looks less convincing on a closer reading. Abraham tithed in Genesis 14, hundreds of years before Moses. Jacob vowed a tithe in Genesis 28, still long before Sinai. In both cases there was no Law, no Levites, no temple system—just worship. Abraham tithed to Melchizedek, a type of Christ, in gratitude for God's blessing. Jacob tithed as a vow of devotion. Then centuries later, the Law simply codified what men of faith were already doing. And in Hebrews 7, the Holy Spirit doesn't argue that tithing ended at the Law—He actually builds an eternal case for Christ's priesthood on Abraham's tithe. If the tithe existed before the Law, and if Jesus affirmed it after the Law, then it cannot be dismissed as a Mosaic relic.

Some critics will raise their hand here and say, "But wait—Acts 15 didn't impose tithing on Gentiles. At the Jerusalem Council, when the apostles sent instructions to the churches, they only listed a handful of essentials: abstain from idols, from blood, from things strangled, and from fornication. If tithing mattered, wouldn't they have included it?" On the surface that sounds compelling, but think it through. The purpose of Acts 15 wasn't to write an entire Christian ethics code. It was to settle one burning question: do Gentiles have to be circumcised and keep the ceremonial law to be saved? The answer was no. So the council gave a short list that would allow Jewish and Gentile believers to share table fellowship without constant offense. That's why the list focuses on food tied to idolatry and immorality—not on the whole counsel of Christian living.

If we reduce Christianity to that list, we're in trouble. Acts 15 doesn't mention generosity. It doesn't mention sexual ethics beyond porneia. It doesn't mention gathering on the Lord's Day. It doesn't mention baptism, prayer, holiness, or a dozen other non-negotiables of the Christian life. So to argue that silence on tithing equals abolition is a too narrow a reading of the passage. The council was answering a narrow question, not handing down a comprehensive rulebook. Cheerful generosity is the ceiling and the spirit; the tithe is a floor.

And when you step outside Acts 15, Paul makes clear what the financial ethic for Gentile believers looks like. In 1 Corinthians 9 he ties the support of gospel workers directly

to the temple tithe, and says *"even so hath the Lord ordained."* In
2 Corinthians 8–9 he paints the picture of grace-filled
generosity that goes beyond the baseline tithe. In Philippians
4 he thanks the church for their sacrificial partnership in
giving, calling it fruit that abounds to their account. In other
words, the New Testament ethic for Gentile believers isn't
silence—it's Spirit-filled stewardship. Acts 15 doesn't erase
tithing. It simply wasn't written to address it. The rest of the
New Testament shows us exactly how God expects Gentile
believers to give: faithfully, proportionately, joyfully, and in
line with the pattern God ordained long before.

2. "I Tithe On My Take Home Pay, not Gross."

Let's deal with a question that comes up often: should
the tithe be calculated before taxes or after taxes?

Scripture is clear on two fronts. First, we are
commanded to pay taxes. Jesus said, *"Render therefore unto
Caesar the things which are Caesar's; and unto God the things that are
God's."* (Matthew 22:21) Caesar was the face of human
government, and Paul later echoed this in Romans 13:
"Render therefore to all their dues: tribute to whom tribute is due."
Taxes are not unscriptural; they are part of honoring God by
honoring the authorities He has placed over us.

But here's the key: taxes do not define what your
increase is. Deuteronomy is clear—the tithe is on what
comes up in the field, not what is counted in the barn after
expenses. The government may reduce your paycheck before
you see it, but it has no authority to redefine what God calls
increase.

Deuteronomy 14:22 puts it bluntly: *"Thou shalt truly tithe all the increase of thy seed, that the field bringeth forth year by year."* Notice three things here. First, the command is absolute— *truly tithe all the increase.* There's no hedging, no partiality. Second, notice the location of the calculation: *the field.* The tithe is determined at the most raw level, right where the crop springs up. It is not recalculated in the barn after storage, spoilage, deductions, or adjustments. God defines the tithe in the field, not in the ledger. Third, notice the time marker: *year by year.* It is systematic, regular, predictable. This was not a sporadic donation but a steady rhythm built into life itself.

Think of it this way. Rent or a mortgage also reduces your spendable money, but no one would argue that paying your landlord shrinks the definition of your increase. The same goes for a car loan or groceries. These are expenses, not determinants of increase. Taxes fall into that same category—an expense you must pay, but not something that reduces what God calls His portion.

If you harvest ten apples and the tax rate is 20%, Caesar rightfully collects two apples. But God still calls for His one apple. Jesus' words are not a sequence—*first Caesar, then God*—but two claims of right. And the very word *render* underscores this. To render is to relinquish what is already owed. You don't render by calculating; you render by paying a rightful claim. So when Jesus says, *"Render unto Caesar… and unto God,"* He is not giving us a formula for which comes first, but affirming that both Caesar and God have legitimate claims.

Even our modern tax systems reflect this. The IRS might

take 20% of your paycheck. Your state taxes might take another 5%. Your city might collect 2%. But notice: each one taxes your gross, not your net. None of them says, "Well, since the IRS already took its share, we'll just tax what's left." No—they all calculate on the gross. Why? Because the gross is your true increase.

The same principle applies to God. If the IRS won't settle for your leftovers, why should the Lord of heaven and earth? Your tithe is on the gross—on the increase as God defines it, not as man reduces it.

Now, what about tax refunds? A refund is not new increase; it's money you already tithed on when you first earned it. If anything, you might view it as a return of what was already God's.

So here's the bottom line: Jesus wasn't giving a formula in Matthew 22; He was establishing rights. Caesar has a rightful claim. God has a rightful claim. Both must be rendered. But only one is holy: *"The tithe… is the LORD's: it is holy unto the LORD."* (Leviticus 27:30)

3. "We're Under Grace, Not Law"

Yes, we are under grace. But grace never lowers God's standards; it raises them. Jesus made this plain in the Sermon on the Mount. The Law said, *"Don't commit adultery,"* but grace presses deeper: *"Don't even lust."* The Law said, *"Don't murder,"* but grace intensifies: *"Don't even hate."* Grace doesn't cancel God's commands—it carries them to their fullest meaning.

That's why when the Pharisees prided themselves on tithing their herbs—mint and cumin—yet neglected justice and mercy, Jesus didn't say, "Stop tithing, you're free from that now." He said, *"These ought ye to have done, and not to leave the other undone."* (Matthew 23:23) In other words: do both. Don't abandon the tithe, and don't miss the heart. That is grace raising the standard—both the heart and the act must be right.

Paul reinforces the same principle when he says, *"Shall we sin because we are not under the law, but under grace? God forbid."* (Romans 6:15) Grace doesn't excuse disobedience; it empowers greater obedience. Grace doesn't make the tithe smaller; it makes our giving bigger, freer, and more joyful.

So the real question isn't, "Does grace cancel the tithe?" It's, "If grace calls us to deeper obedience in every other area, why would it suddenly call us to less in our giving?" If the Law brought a tenth, grace invites us to bring the tithe with a glad heart and then overflow beyond it in generosity. Grace doesn't loosen our hands from giving—it loosens our hearts to give more.

4.   "The New Testament Doesn't Explicitly Command Tithing"

It doesn't need to. The New Testament assumes it.

In 1 Corinthians 16, Paul instructs believers to set aside their giving on the first day of the week, in the assembly. That's not random generosity—it's structured, rhythmic, and in line with the firstfruits principle. In 1 Corinthians 9, Paul ties gospel ministry directly to the principle of the temple tithe, and then seals it with these words: *"Even so hath the Lord ordained."* (1 Corinthians 9:14) That's not suggestion; that's continuity. Hebrews 7 goes even deeper, building theology on Abraham's tithe, showing that Christ Himself, through the order of Melchizedek, still receives tithes.

The New Testament doesn't reprint every Old Testament command verbatim, and it often carries forward moral truth by principle and pattern—not by restating every line. For example, we don't see repeated commands for honoring parents, avoiding idols, or keeping ourselves from murder—but no one suggests those commands have expired. The same principle applies here. Unless Scripture clearly shows that something is fulfilled in Christ (as with the sacrificial system), it continues.

The burden of proof, then, doesn't lie on the believer who honors God with the tithe, but on the one who insists it has disappeared. Grace doesn't reduce God's call; it deepens it. The New Testament assumes tithing not as a minimum tax, but as a holy rhythm carried forward into the life of the church.

5. "Tithing Is Just an Old Testament Ritual Like Sacrifices"

It's true that sacrifices ended at the cross. Every lamb, every goat, every altar pointed forward to Christ, the Lamb of God who takes away the sin of the world. When He cried, *"It is finished,"* the sacrificial system was fulfilled once for all. That's why we don't bring bulls and goats to the church parking lot on Sunday. The shadow gave way to the substance.

But the tithe is not rooted in the blood of animals. It is rooted in the ownership of God. *"The earth is the LORD's, and the fulness thereof."* (Psalm 24:1) That hasn't changed. Long before Moses ever wrote a line of law, Abraham tithed to Melchizedek, and Jacob vowed a tithe at Bethel. These weren't ritual acts tied to temple sacrifices; they were worship acts tied to God's authority as Creator and Owner.

Hebrews 7 makes this crystal clear. The writer takes us back to Abraham's tithe to Melchizedek and shows that Christ's priesthood is patterned after that same eternal order. In other words, the tithe was not swallowed up by the cross—it was carried forward to Christ Himself. Sacrifices ceased because they were fulfilled in Him. The tithe continues because He still reigns, still receives, and still owns it all.

So the comparison between tithing and sacrifices is a false one. Sacrifices were temporary shadows; the tithe is a permanent acknowledgment of God's ownership. One ended because Christ paid the final price. The other continues because Christ is Lord over every paycheck, every field, every account.

6. "Jesus Rebuked the Pharisees for Tithing"

It's true that Jesus rebuked the Pharisees—but not because they tithed. His concern was their hypocrisy. They were meticulous about measuring out herbs and spices to the very leaf, but at the same time, they neglected the weightier matters of the law: justice, mercy, and faith (Matthew 23:23).

Jesus called that hypocrisy, and rightly so. But notice what He did say: *"These ought ye to have done, and not to leave the other undone."* In other words, the problem wasn't their tithing; the problem was that they thought tithing excused them from compassion and righteousness.

If Jesus had wanted to abolish the tithe, that moment was tailor-made for it. Instead, He affirmed it. He told them to keep bringing their tithe—but to do it with hearts that also practiced mercy and justice. That's not a dismissal of tithing; that's a call to deeper discipleship.

So when someone says, "Jesus rebuked the Pharisees for tithing," the truth is gentler but stronger: He rebuked them for doing it without love. The tithe itself remained intact. The lesson for us is not to abandon the tithe, but to bring it with a heart that is right before God.

7. "My Increase Is Just Spiritual, Not Financial"

That may sound humble, but it's not what Scripture says. When the Bible defines increase, it always does so in material terms. Leviticus 27 speaks of seed, cattle, and the fruit of the land. Deuteronomy 14 lists corn, wine, and oil. These were the financial engines of an agrarian economy. In the New Testament, Paul tells the Corinthians to give *"as God hath prospered him."* (1 Corinthians 16:2) That prosperity isn't mystical—it's the paycheck, the harvest, the goods in your hand.

Now, does God also give spiritual increase? Absolutely. Ephesians 1 says we are *"blessed with all spiritual blessings in heavenly places in Christ."* But notice: those blessings fuel worship, generosity, and joy—they don't cancel financial increase. The tithe was never about spiritual maturity points; it was about acknowledging God's ownership in the realm of daily provision.

So let's keep the categories straight. Spiritual blessings call us to gratitude. Financial blessings enlarge our resources. The firstfruits principle ties directly to the latter. If your paycheck went up, you had increase. If your business earned a profit, you had increase. Scripture doesn't redefine those gains as "just spiritual" in order to sidestep obedience.

The truth is, spiritual blessings and material increase belong together. One fills the heart with thanks; the other fills the hands with provision. And both call us to return to the Lord with joy.

8. "I Can Tithe Wherever I Want"

Scripture directs the tithe first to the local church. From the beginning, God was specific about where His tithe belonged. In Deuteronomy 12, He told Israel they could not just pick their own place or preference: *"But unto the place which the LORD your God shall choose… thither ye shall bring your burnt offerings, and your sacrifices, and your tithes."* (Deuteronomy 12:5-6) The tithe was not a free-floating donation; it was to be brought to the house where God placed His name.

In the New Testament, that principle continues. Paul calls the church *"the house of God, which is the church of the living God, the pillar and ground of the truth."* (1 Timothy 3:15) The storehouse of Malachi corresponds today to the local church—the gathered body where you worship, are shepherded, and join hands in mission. That's where the Lord's portion belongs.

Now, does that mean you can't give elsewhere? Of course not. Scripture is full of other giving: offerings for the poor, support for missionaries, gifts to bless others. Those are beautiful and necessary. But they are offerings, not the tithe. The tithe is God's portion, already marked as holy. Redirecting it to a charity, a podcast, or even a missionary you love doesn't change its label—it's still *"the LORD's."* To divert it is to misapply it, like using someone else's money for your own plans. Malachi doesn't soften the word: to withhold or misdirect the tithe is to rob God (Malachi 3:8-10).

This isn't about church budgets or fundraising—it's about faithfulness. The Lord has not left this open-ended. He said where His tithe belongs. Our part is not to renegotiate the terms but to obey with joy. The offerings that flow above and beyond the tithe can go a hundred places, but the tithe itself belongs in the storehouse of God.

9. "I Can't Afford to Tithe"

I know money can feel tight. Still, Scripture invites us to trust God first—and promises His care. And Malachi 3 doesn't flatter us here. It calls those who withhold the tithe *"robbers"* of God, and it says they are *"cursed with a curse."* Then it does something remarkable—it challenges us to test God in this very thing: *"Prove me now herewith…if I will not open you the windows of heaven, and pour you out a blessing."* (Malachi 3:10) The issue isn't math; it's trust. When someone says, 'I can't

ANSWERING THE TOP 15 OBJECTIONS

afford it,' often the deeper struggle is trust. Budgets rarely look like they can handle a tithe at first. But Scripture calls us to put God first and trust Him to supply (1 Kings 17; Malachi 3:10). The issue isn't math—it's whether we believe His promise to care for us. That's why tithing becomes an exercise in faith, not just finance.

Think of it this way: the numbers will never line up on their own. If you wait until your budget feels comfortable, you will never start. The tithe is not funded by surplus; it is fueled by faith. Elijah's widow in 1 Kings 17 thought she had only one more meal left. But she obeyed, gave first, and found that the barrel of meal never wasted and the cruse of oil never failed. God's promise has always been: "Put Me first, and I will supply."

Now, let's be clear: Christ bore the curse of the Law at the cross. Tithing is not a way of "buying" salvation or purchasing blessing. But that doesn't erase the Father's discipline (Hebrews 12), nor does it undo the sowing-and-reaping principle Paul lays out in 2 Corinthians 9:6–11 and Galatians 6:7–10. We're not slot-machine givers pulling for payout—we're disciples walking with the grain of God's world.

I've seen it time and again in my own life and in others'. The ones who say, "I can't afford it," usually stay stuck. The ones who say, "I will trust God and obey Him first," almost always have stories to tell of how He met them, sometimes in ways they never could have scripted. Sometimes it's abundance, sometimes it's sufficiency, sometimes it's protection from losses they never saw coming. But the testimony rings the same: "I thought I couldn't afford it, but

I couldn't afford not to."

So when you face this objection in your own heart, remember this: you will always serve one master or the other—fear or faith. Tithing is the Lord's way of training our hearts to serve faith. And when you trust Him with the first tenth, you will find that He knows how to stretch the ninety in ways no spreadsheet ever could.

10. "I Already Gave in Other Ways"

This is one of the most common confusions—and one of the most dangerous. Offerings are not tithes. Scripture makes the distinction plain. Malachi 3 says, *"Ye have robbed me…in tithes and offerings."* Two categories, not one. The tithe is God's portion; offerings are our overflow. The tithe is the baseline of obedience; offerings are the outpouring of generosity.

So when someone says, "I already gave in other ways," what they usually mean is that they redirected God's tithe to some other good cause. Maybe they helped a missionary, gave to a charity, paid for a neighbor's groceries, or even slipped money to their pastor directly. Those are all beautiful acts of love, but they do not replace the tithe. The tithe is holy unto the Lord. It belongs in the storehouse. To use it for something else—even something good—is to misappropriate what God has already claimed for Himself.

Think of it like this: if you were entrusted with funds at work that were earmarked for payroll, you wouldn't be free to spend them on office furniture, even if the office badly needed it. It wouldn't matter that the purchase was good or that the company benefited. The money had a designated purpose. To use it otherwise would be theft, not generosity. In the same way, God has marked out the first tenth as His, for His house. To withhold it is robbery. To reroute it is mismanagement.

That doesn't mean you shouldn't give offerings. In fact, offerings above the tithe are where generosity blossoms. Supporting missionaries, meeting needs in your community, giving to charities, or helping friends in crisis—all of these are part of New Testament giving. But they are in addition to the tithe, not instead of it. The tithe is the floor; offerings are the ceiling.

The truth is, if we confuse the two, we rob both. We rob God of what He calls holy, and we rob ourselves of the joy of true overflow giving. When we keep them distinct—tithe first, offerings after—the heart is freed to give without guilt, and the house of God is supplied for its mission.

So yes, give in many ways. Be generous on every occasion. But don't mistake offerings for obedience. Start with the tithe. Then let love overflow.

11. "The Tithe Was Food, Not Money"

Today our increase is wages, not wheat. The principle remains: ten percent of increase, whether that increase is fruit, flocks, or a paycheck.

Some readers will point out, "But the Old Testament doesn't just have one tithe. There's the Levitical tithe (Numbers 18), the festival tithe (Deuteronomy 14), and the poor tithe (Deuteronomy 26). Doesn't that mean Israel gave

20–30%, not a single 10%?"

It's true that Old Testament Israel had several structured tithes. But notice how they function: the *first tenth*—the Lord's portion—was always fixed. That belonged to Him and went to sustain the Levites. Then, on top of that, God added cycles of generosity for feasts and for the poor. In other words, the first tenth was the baseline. The festival and poor tithes looked a lot like what we would now call *offerings* and *alms*.

That's why in the New Testament, the principle of the first tenth continues as holy to the Lord (Leviticus 27:30; 1 Corinthians 9:14; Hebrews 7:8). Then we also see offerings for gospel work (Philippians 4), alms for the needy (Matthew 6; Acts 6), and even sacrificial generosity far above the baseline (2 Corinthians 8–9). The categories didn't vanish— they reappeared, reshaped.

So when I speak of the tithe today as "ten percent," I'm not flattening three systems into one. I'm saying the first tenth remains the Lord's portion, while the rest of Scripture still calls us to overflow with offerings and alms. The baseline remains; the generosity expands. That's why the "three tithes = 30%" "gotcha" doesn't actually undo the argument—it reinforces it. God has always set apart His holy portion, and He has always called His people to go beyond it.

12. "The Church Just Wants My Money"

That objection sounds modern, but it's as old as Cain. It reveals a heart problem, not a church budget problem. The tithe doesn't belong to the church. It belongs to the Lord.

Leviticus 27:30 is clear: "*The tithe is the LORD's: it is holy unto the LORD.*" The church is simply the storehouse, the steward God appointed. Paul said it plainly in 1 Corinthians 9:14: "*Even so hath the Lord ordained that they which preach the gospel should live of the gospel.*" It's God's design, not man's invention. Refusing to tithe because you distrust people is really refusing to tithe because you distrust God's order.

And let's be honest: if the church truly were after your money, God gave you the perfect out—don't give to men, give to Him. The tithe is an act of worship. You are not tipping a pastor; you are honoring the King. If the leadership is unfaithful, God will deal with them. But your obedience isn't diminished by their flaws. It's holy because it belongs to Him, not them.

When someone says, 'The church just wants my money,' I understand the concern. Sadly, some churches have misused funds, and that creates real distrust. But Scripture reminds us that the tithe is the Lord's, not the pastor's or the budget's (Leviticus 27:30). The church is simply the steward. So the deeper question is not about men but about God's design. If leadership fails, He will hold them accountable. But your act of giving remains holy because it belongs to Him, not them. In that light, the real danger is letting distrust of people keep us from trusting God's order. The issue isn't ultimately money—it's worship.

Some even state that early church history shows tithing was not part of the normal practice and that the modern church "snuck" it in. I've avoided building this case on church history for a reason. History is helpful, but it's not inspired; it's written by people like us, with partial records and mixed angles. Scripture is our final authority. Where the Bible speaks plainly—about increase, firstfruits, the storehouse, and *"even so hath the Lord ordained"*—I don't need a later document to overrule it.

As for the "Trojan horse" claim—that tithing slipped into the church to smuggle in control—I see the opposite in Nehemiah. The real Trojan horse was withholding. Leave the store room empty and an enemy will occupy it. Tithing didn't smuggle legalism into grace; neglect smuggled famine into worship. If we must choose a posture, let it be the one that keeps the chambers full and the Levites at their posts.

13. "Pastors Shouldn't Be Paid"

This objection surfaces often, usually cloaked in piety but rooted in misunderstanding. The idea goes something like this: "If pastors are truly called by God, they shouldn't take money for it." It sounds spiritual, but it isn't biblical.

Paul tackles this head-on in 1 Corinthians 9. He draws a series of plain analogies: soldiers don't go to war at their own expense, farmers eat from their crops, shepherds drink from the flock. Then he makes the comparison inescapable: *"Even so hath the Lord ordained that they which preach the gospel should live of the gospel."* (1 Corinthians 9:14) That phrase—*even so hath the Lord ordained*—is as strong as Scripture gets. This is not Paul's opinion or a cultural quirk. It is God's ordinance.

And Paul roots it, not in clever reasoning, but in Scripture itself. He quotes Deuteronomy: *"Thou shalt not muzzle the ox that treadeth out the corn."* The principle is clear:

the worker is sustained by his work. If God cares enough about an ox to ensure it eats while laboring, how much more about His servants who labor in the Word?

The Old Testament pattern was the same. The Levites did not farm fields or herd cattle; they lived on the tithes brought into the storehouse. That wasn't greed; it was God's design. The tithe sustained the temple so that ministry could happen without distraction. Paul says the same pattern carries forward into the church. The gospel ministry is not meant to run on fumes or side jobs—it is meant to be sustained by God's people, through God's appointed means.

To call pastoral support 'greedy' misunderstands God's design. Scripture shows that supporting those who labor in the Word is His provision, not man's ambition (1 Corinthians 9:14; 1 Timothy 5:17-18). Of course, pastors must model integrity, and abuses must be corrected. But the principle itself is not greed—it is God's appointed means for gospel work. Scripture condemns hirelings who exploit the flock. But the answer to abuse is not starvation. The answer is faithful oversight, generous giving, and pastors who live what they preach.

When believers withhold the tithe because they bristle at pastoral pay, they are not making a statement against men—they are pushing back against God's ordinance. The tithe is not "for the pastor." It is the Lord's, brought into His storehouse. He has chosen to supply His servants through it. To support pastors, then, is not charity; it is obedience. And to refuse is not frugality; it is disobedience.

The point is not to enrich men but to free them—to let shepherds shepherd without distraction, to let ministers

minister without moonlighting. A church that honors this
ordinance will find its leaders more devoted, its ministry
more fruitful, and its people more blessed. That's not man's
design; that's God's.

14. "Tithing Is Legalism"

This objection rests on a confusion of terms. Legalism is
the teaching that you must add works to faith in order to be
saved. That's not what tithing is. Tithing has never been
about earning salvation—it has always been about expressing
worship.

Think about Abraham. He wasn't under the Law; Sinai
hadn't even smoked yet. And yet when God blessed him
through Melchizedek, he gave a tenth in faith and gratitude.
That was not legalism—it was worship. Jacob, too, tithed at
Bethel in devotion, long before Moses ever carried tablets
down a mountain. Israel tithed under the Law as an act of
obedience, not as a way to purchase salvation. Jesus Himself
affirmed the tithe in Matthew 23:23, not as a path to
righteousness but as part of a life rightly ordered before God.
Paul carried the principle into the church in 1 Corinthians 9,
and Hebrews 7 magnifies it under the eternal priesthood of
Christ. None of that smacks of legalism. It is holiness, rooted
in the recognition that "the tithe is the Lord's."

To call obedience legalism is to twist the meaning of
grace. Grace doesn't abolish God's commands—it empowers
joyful obedience to them. Grace doesn't say, "Don't worry
about honoring God with your substance." Grace says,
"Now that you've been redeemed, your whole life belongs to

Him." Grace makes giving a delight, not a debt. It lifts the standard, just as Jesus did in the Sermon on the Mount, where He deepened every command into the heart.

So tithing is not legalism; it is lordship. It is not bondage; it is freedom from the grip of mammon. It is not a way of trying to buy God's favor; it is a way of confessing that His favor has already been poured out on you in Christ. When you bring the firstfruits with joy, you are not trying to get saved—you are celebrating that you are saved.

The real danger is not legalism but license. It's using grace as an excuse to withhold what God has declared holy. Grace doesn't weaken our devotion; it strengthens it. And when you see it that way, the tithe isn't a chain around your neck; it's an anchor for your heart, keeping you steady in worship and trust.

15. "God Doesn't Need My Money"

That is absolutely true. God owns the cattle on a thousand hills (Psalm 50:10). He owns the hills themselves. He spoke the universe into existence and sustains it with His word. The One who created gold does not need yours to fund His kingdom. If He wanted, He could multiply loaves and fishes every Sunday. He doesn't command the tithe because He is running short.

So why does He command it? Because it reveals your heart. The tithe was never about financing God—it was about forming us. Leviticus 27 says the tithe is holy to the Lord. Malachi calls it robbery when withheld. Jesus affirms it as obedience, not because God has a budget shortfall, but because He knows that money is the chief rival for our trust. The tithe exposes whether I truly believe Psalm 24:1: *"The earth is the LORD's, and the fulness thereof."*

Think of it this way: if God doesn't need my money but still commands my tithe, then the only purpose left is to test whether I will glorify Him and give thanks. It's not about God's need; it's about my worship. The tithe becomes a thermometer, taking the temperature of my heart. Do I really believe He is Lord over all, or do I live as though I am?

When you bring the tithe, you're not funding God— you're confessing God. You're saying, "Lord, all I have is Thine. I trust You, I thank You, and I honor You first." That posture of glory and thanks is what Romans 1 says mankind lost in its fall, and what the gospel restores. The tithe simply gives it hands and feet.

So yes, God doesn't need your money. But you need to tithe. Not for His lack, but for your health. Because in those firstfruits, you train your soul to bow and to bless, to dethrone mammon and enthrone Christ. And that's the point—not that God gains revenue, but that His people gain reverence.

Wrapping it Up

Some say, "There is no requirement to tithe—only to give freely." But if grace truly abounds, why spend energy writing against the floor? If the Spirit moves us far beyond ten percent, then a baseline cannot restrain us—it can only steady us. To argue away the floor is, in practice, to argue downward. Removing it does not raise generosity; it more often excuses withholding.

Even everyday life shows this principle. When Panera piloted "Panera Cares," it removed posted prices and let customers pay what they wished. After nine years, the final café closed in 2019, with Panera admitting the concept was "no longer viable."[10] The floor didn't inspire most people to go higher; it drained the whole system. It's an imperfect analogy, but it illustrates a human tendency: removing floors often reduces participation, not raises it.

So I know why I write to uphold the tithe: because a confessed portion belongs to the Lord, because Scripture never repeals His ordinance, and because the church needs steady means for its God-ordained purpose. But I truly wonder—why spend your time and resources arguing that God's people don't owe Him firstfruits, especially if you still want them to give generously? If grace really leads us above the tithe, then a baseline can't harm you. It can only help anchor the ordinary saints in worship and let grace run beyond it.

[10] https://www.eater.com/2019/2/5/18212499/panera-cares-closing-pay-what-you-can-restaurant

CHAPTER NINE

OTHER PRINCIPLES OF GIVING IN THE BIBLE

"The tithe is the floor, not the ceiling—Scripture calls us higher, to firstfruits, offerings, alms, and generosity that overflows."

By this point we've seen that the tithe is not an Old Testament relic but a New Testament reality—anchored before the Law, codified under the Law, reaffirmed by Christ, ordained in the church, and still received by the living Christ Himself. But the tithe isn't the whole story. It's the baseline. The rest of Scripture is pulsing with principles that orbit around it—principles that show giving is not just about math, but about the heart, about worship, about God's glory and our good.

The Bible often uses the word *firstfruits* alongside the tithe. Proverbs 3:9-10 says, *"Honour the LORD with thy*

113

substance, and with the firstfruits of all thine increase: so shall thy barns be filled with plenty, and thy presses shall burst out with new wine." Firstfruits meant God first. Before the farmer ate a meal, before he sold a crop, before he enjoyed the fruit of his own labor, he acknowledged that it all came from God by giving Him the first portion. The principle is as clear today as it was then. Who gets the first cut of your increase—the Lord or the IRS? The Lord or your mortgage? The Lord or your spending plan? Firstfruits has always meant God first, not God last.

Some readers might point out that the Bible uses the words *tithe* and *firstfruits* differently. And that's true. They are not identical terms. The tithe is a proportion—a tenth of all increase, holy unto the Lord. The firstfruits, on the other hand, were about priority—the very first portion of the harvest, the first cut of the crop, the first sheaf brought to God before anything else was eaten or sold. One is about the amount; the other is about the order.

But notice how seamlessly the two principles work together. God never wanted just a tenth at any point in the year. He wanted the first tenth. Firstfruits showed His priority. The tithe showed His portion. Together they formed a posture of the heart: "God gets His part, and God gets it first."

That's exactly the principle carried into the New Testament. Paul says in 1 Corinthians 16, *"Upon the first day of the week let every one of you lay by him in store, as God hath prospered him."* There it is again: priority and proportion. God gets it first ("the first day"), and God gets it as He has prospered you ("the proportion"). The same pulse runs through

Proverbs 3:9-10: *"Honour the LORD with thy substance, and with the firstfruits of all thine increase: so shall thy barns be filled with plenty."* Firstfruits—priority. All thine increase—proportion.

So we don't collapse the terms into one. Firstfruits are distinct from the tithe, but they are aligned principles, and both are assumed in New Testament giving. We put God first in order (priority), and we put God first in portion (proportion). And the result is the same promise Proverbs held out: God fills the barns, bursts the presses, and proves Himself faithful.

There is also the principle of *freewill offerings*. These were above and beyond the tithe. Exodus 35 tells how the people brought so much for the tabernacle that Moses finally had to tell them to stop giving. Imagine that problem—too much generosity! That wasn't tithe; that was overflow. The tithe was the baseline, but the freewill offering was love poured out. And Paul echoes the same in 2 Corinthians 8-9 when he speaks of grace giving that abounds out of joy and even poverty. The Macedonians gave *"beyond their power."* That's the same pulse as Exodus—the overflow of hearts set aflame with love for God.

Then there is *alms*. Proverbs 19:17 says, *"He that hath pity upon the poor lendeth unto the LORD; and that which he hath given will he pay him again."* Jesus assumed His disciples would give alms (Matthew 6:1-4), but He warned them not to do it for show. Alms are mercy-gifts to the needy. They are distinct from the tithe, distinct from freewill offerings, but they carry the same principle—what you do with your substance reveals whether your heart is full of glory and thanks or not.

Another principle that runs all through Scripture is

stewardship. Paul says in 1 Corinthians 4:2, *"Moreover it is required in stewards, that a man be found faithful."* You don't own anything—you're a steward. Everything in your account, your wallet, your business, your home, your land, your investments, even your body and breath—all of it is God's. That changes the posture of giving. You're not deciding what percentage of your money to give to God. You're deciding how much of God's money to keep for yourself.

Jesus also made it clear that giving *dethrones mammon*. *"Ye cannot serve God and mammon."* (Matthew 6:24) Money is always trying to be your master. The tithe and offering are God's way of cutting mammon down to size. When you hand over the firstfruits, when you give with joy, you are saying to mammon, "You don't own me. You don't rule me. I serve God." Giving isn't just about supporting ministry. It's about breaking money's grip on your soul.

Paul adds another word to the giving vocabulary: *simplicity*, which means generosity or single-heartedness. In Romans 12:8 he says, *"he that giveth, let him do it with simplicity."* In 2 Corinthians 9 he says our giving spreads *"bountifulness"* and thanksgiving to God. The New Testament words for giving are overflowing with joy, cheerfulness, liberality. You never get the sense of tight-fisted accounting. You get the sense of open hands and open hearts.

The widow's mite in Mark 12 reminds us that the measure of giving is not in the amount but in the sacrifice. She gave all her living, and Jesus said she gave more than all the rich men dropping their bags of gold. Zacchaeus in Luke 19 proves the same: when salvation came to his house, his wallet changed. He stood up and said, *"Behold, Lord, the half of my goods I give to the poor."* He didn't do that to get saved; he did it because he was saved. Real salvation bends the knee and opens the hand.

The flip side is the rich fool in Luke 12. He built bigger barns, hoarded for himself, and said to his soul, *"Take thine ease."* God called him a fool because he was not *"rich toward God."* That's the real issue. Are you rich toward yourself or rich toward God? Tithing and giving are the thermometer that answers the question.

The early church in Acts took this pulse and turned it into practice. Believers sold houses and lands. They laid the proceeds at the apostles' feet. Barnabas sold a field. Ananias and Sapphira lied about theirs and paid with their lives. The message is plain: giving was serious business, holy business, God's business.

The Philippian church gave sacrificially to Paul, and he told them in Philippians 4:17 that *"fruit may abound to your account."* That's the mystery of giving. It looks like subtraction, but in heaven it's addition. It looks like loss, but Paul calls it fruit on your eternal ledger.

And don't miss this: in Numbers 18, even the Levites tithed. The leaders weren't exempt. They gave too, because giving itself is worship. Pastors today are not exempt. They, too, are stewards. They, too, need to bow their hearts by opening their hands. No one is above worship.

So when you gather all these threads—firstfruits, freewill offerings, alms, stewardship, mammon, simplicity, cheerful generosity, widow's mites, Zacchaeus, rich fools, Acts believers, Philippian partners, priestly tithes—you see the same pulse. Giving is not about technicalities. It's about trust.

Not about math. About glory and thanks. Not about what God needs, but about what God deserves.

The tithe is the baseline. The rest of the Bible says don't stop there. Give with firstfruits priority, with freewill love, with merciful alms, with cheerful simplicity, with stewardship faithfulness, with mammon dethroned, with joy in the Spirit. Because the God who gave His only begotten Son deserves no less than our open hands and our overflowing hearts.

CHAPTER TEN

CONCLUSION – BOWED HEARTS, OPEN HANDS

"Tithing is a thermometer – it doesn't set your spiritual temperature—it just reveals it."

When we started, I told you about "dirty paper." Money has no life of its own, but it finds the pulse of yours. It does not create a temperature; it simply reveals one. And what it reveals is not trivial—it tells the truth about your hinge. Romans 1 showed us the hinge where mankind fell: *"They glorified him not as God, neither were thankful."* The gospel swings that hinge back. To believe is to bow low in glory and to rise up in thanksgiving. That is the posture of a redeemed heart.

The tithe simply makes that posture visible. It is not a tax. It is not a buy-in. It is a thermometer. A thermometer doesn't cure the fever, but it shows whether health is present.

And the reading is clear: a bowed heart and a grateful soul never resent moving a decimal point to honor the Lord. In fact, such a heart will often give far more than ten percent— not because it has to, but because it loves to. The tithe is the floor, not the ceiling.

I've seen this not only in Scripture, but in my own life. Over ten years, I kept a personal journal—sixty pages of prayers, reflections, highs and lows. Out of curiosity, I asked an AI tool to "score" my joy year by year. Then I compared it to my giving records. With 90% confidence, the AI found a simple pattern: when joy rose one year, my giving as a percentage of income rose the next. I didn't plan that. I didn't see it at the time. But even a cold algorithm confirmed what the Bible had already said: joy and generosity travel together. Glory and thanks are not theory—they show up in what we do with God's portion.

So here is where this book ends and your obedience begins. The tithe is not about funding God, as if the Ancient of Days were running short. The tithe is about forming you. It bends the knees. It opens the hands. It dethrones the god of "mine" and retrains the soul to say, week after week, "Thou art greater. All is Thine. I gladly return what is holy unto Thee."

Do not let this be a book you nodded through and shelved. Let it be a hinge you oiled and swung. Start where Scripture starts: God owns it all. Confess it. The tithe is holy. Set it apart. The storehouse is God's house. Bring it there. The timing is first. Honor Him off the top. The spirit is joy. God loves a cheerful giver. And then, beyond the baseline, let grace run free—offerings, alms, generosity without calculation. If the cross has taken your sin, let gratitude take your grip.

And if you've been afraid, hear Malachi's dare: *"Prove me now."* Not slot-machine theology, but Fatherly promise. Sometimes His blessing comes as supply. Sometimes as sufficiency. Sometimes as protection from devourers you never knew were circling. But always as joy—the joy of walking in step with Him.

So let's end where we began: glory and thanks. Bow low before the Lord. Say with Abraham, *"Thou art greater."* Say with Jacob, *"Of all that Thou shalt give me I will surely give the tenth unto Thee."* Say with the Macedonians, *"In deep poverty our joy abounds."* Say with Paul, *"Even so hath the Lord ordained."* Say with Malachi, *"We will bring all the tithes into the storehouse."*

And then do it—not grudgingly, not anxiously, but gladly. Because Christ lives to receive it.

Take a pen. Take your budget. Take your heart. Draw the line that should have been there all along. Make the tithe the baseline, and worship the anthem. Put God first—today, this week, this month, and for the rest of your life—until it becomes the rhythm your children assume and your grandchildren inherit.

Let your "dirty paper" tell the truth about your soul: that the hinge has swung, that Jesus is Lord, and that you are, by grace, a glad and grateful steward.

"Blessed be the Lord, who daily loadeth us with benefits, even the God of our salvation." (Psalm 68:19) Amen.

ONE LAST WORD

Friend, if you've read this far and you don't know for sure that you're saved, don't close this book without settling it. Life is short, eternity is long, and Christ has already paid the price for your sins on the cross.

The Bible says, *"Behold, now is the accepted time; behold, now is the day of salvation."* (2 Corinthians 6:2) Don't put it off. Don't wait for a better time. There may not be one.

Right now, turn from your sin and trust Jesus Christ alone as your Saviour. Call upon Him in faith, and He will save you. That's His promise.